EVERYWHERE PRESENT

*Christianity in a
One-Storey Universe*

STEPHEN FREEMAN

CONCILIAR PRESS
CHESTERTON, INDIANA

EVERYWHERE PRESENT:
Christianity in a One-Storey Universe

Copyright © 2010 by Stephen Freeman

All rights reserved. Printed in the United States of America

Published by Conciliar Media Ministries
PO Box 748, Chesterton, IN 46304

ISBN 10: 1-936270-10-2
ISBN 13: 978-1-936270-10-1

CONTENTS

for my beloved family

FOREWORD

Fr. Stephen Freeman's excellent book is the story of how faith in our society has been compromised by secularism. What had been an integrated vision of God and humankind, of the divine and the created, in the "one-storey universe" has become a dualistic segregation of God from human life in the "two-storey" model, in which God is absent from the first floor, and people begin to wonder if there is Anyone home up there. Fr. Stephen's presentation analyzes, in a wonderful narrative style, all the various aspects of the loss of the consciousness of the Presence of God in our world. God has not disappeared from our world, but we have tried to exile Him to the second floor.

One of the most fundamental principles of the Christian vision of reality is that God is present everywhere, filling all things. This underlies the essential Christian task of becoming consciously aware of that Presence and bringing that awareness into every aspect of our life. Secularism is the compartmentalization of God and religion, and everything else, into autonomous and unrelated parts of our lives. Secularism does not deny that God exists, but rather states that He has His place and does not necessarily affect other areas of our lives. But soon that compartmentalization leads to an exclusion of God altogether, as we create a world in which we live by our own reasonings. Thus is born a kind of Christian atheism, where we operate as if

God were absent, perhaps even nonexistent. This kind of functional atheism then degrades into faithlessness.

The real Christian task is to integrate our lives and our consciousness by the awareness of God, to overcome the compartmentalization dictated by our culture, and to sanctify all creation by the remembrance of God, awareness of His Presence. In truth, there is nothing that is not permeated by God, and there is nowhere we can flee from the Presence. We live, as it were, in the womb of God. It is not God who has absented Himself from our awareness. Rather, we have shut Him out and become forgetful of His Presence, intentionally oblivious to Reality Himself.

We are faced with the task of overcoming the delusion of our own autonomy and surrendering to Him who rules over all things. Indeed, the compartmentalized world is a delusion of our own creation. It is the ascendancy of the rational mind over spiritual intuition, of the head over the heart. It creates a comfortable world with the safe borders of our own very limited perceptions and narrow vision, an illusion that we can understand and control, because it is not God who created it. When the boundaries crumble and we lose control of our fantasy world, which is as inevitable as death, then perhaps we can begin to deal with Reality Himself and the world as it is. This disillusionment is essential, albeit painful. Only then can we throw off the bondage of the limitations of our sensual perception and rational comprehension. Only then does God break through and awaken us from the dream world of our own fantasies.

It is very chic to declare oneself an atheist, to go with the flow of one or another popular fad of thinly clothed rebellion, and to stand courageously for the pathetic assertion of one's egocentric little world-concept. The comfortable atheism of the schools and universities soon crumbles, and life without God becomes terrifying. Without faith, without spiritual vision and intuition of God, there is only despair. It is this despair that grips our society. Are we too afraid that Grandma may have been right as she trudged to church for those long sermons or endless services? Can we admit that our own vision of reality, our own understanding, may not be adequate? Can we even admit that there might be a reality beyond what we are able to touch and to measure? Do we think we can obliterate our conscience by cutting off our life, the ultimate act of despair?

How tragic it is that so much of the popular version of Christianity preaches a secularized message. It keeps God isolated, but popping in from time to time. It has lost the sense of the permeation of matter by divine Grace, the sacramental vision of reality; it insists that the Eucharist is just bread and wine, baptism is just a bath, and the world operates independently of God. It preaches a moralism of being "good," leading only to obsession with guilt, and then, when that becomes too much, to shamelessness. It preaches that our salvation is acquired by a simple confession, and that it consists of going to "heaven" instead of going to "hell"—not a life lived in cooperation with divine grace, a body, mind, and heart sanctified by the Presence, which, having been "born again by water and the Spirit" in baptism, will continue to live forever, surviving death itself, to be resurrected.

The Christian way, as the Orthodox Tradition understands it, is the path to true freedom, to living in reality as it is, to perceiving the Truth. We understand that our rational minds are limited, and our perception is limited. Thus, we are free to stand before the infinite abyss of the Mystery of God in silence. We don't have to define it; we don't have to describe it. It simply Is. Or rather, He simply Is. And the whole creation shimmers with His glory, and sings the hymn of praise to God. If we follow this way, it gives us ears to hear the cosmic hymn of thanksgiving, and a voice to join in; it gives us eyes to perceive, and

EVERYWHERE PRESENT

senses to taste and smell, and intuitive knowledge that God is Present, and all things exist in Him, and that our salvation and eternal life is to be conscious in Him.

+ JONAH

METROPOLITAN OF ALL AMERICA AND CANADA (OCA)

CHAPTER ONE

THE SHAPE OF THE UNIVERSE

O Heavenly King, the Comforter, the Spirit of Truth,
Who art everywhere present and fillest all things,
Come and abide in us,
Cleanse us from all impurity,
And save our souls, O Good One.

(From the Orthodox Trisagion Prayers)

I spent my childhood in the 1950s and 60s in the semi-rural South. It was a fairly homogeneous culture, marked by its memory of the past (often quite dark) and its hope for a future in the "New South." Such a future was defined by little except prosperity. Everyone hoped for prosperity. The culture was also marked by religion—Protestant almost without exception, and predominantly Baptist. It was in that context that I first came to believe in God. Though I had an idea of God in which I believed, I had no immediate sense of God in the world itself. There was a great disconnect between the God in whom I believed and almost everything around me.

Many of my earliest religious memories are connected with funerals. I came from a large extended family, all of whom lived in the same county. It was inevitable that death would visit my family on a regular basis. Funerals themselves were primarily directed to the living. The dead were respectfully laid to rest. Displays of strong emotion were discouraged. The day of a funeral often concluded with a long covered-dish dinner at my grandparents', at which children played as always and conversation moved quickly to its perennial subjects: family, farming, and automobiles.

When the dead were buried, they were generally dead and gone. There was little conversation about heaven, even less about hell. The Protestant world had no purgatory; thus no further thought was given to the departed other than to offer comfort to those who felt their loss most keenly. There were no services to pray for their souls, no candles to be lit, and no conversation about their eternal disposition. Death brought an end to this life, and though we were taught to believe in a life after death, our experience was often an emptiness with no thoughts to fill the void.

There was an unspoken distance between the living and the dead, and nothing was to disturb it. No one seemed to notice that God Himself was separated from us by the same distance.

What was clear in all this was the finality of death. There was an unspoken distance between the living and the dead, and nothing was to disturb it. No one seemed to notice that God Himself was separated from us by the same distance. For if the dead are with Jesus and are now at an unspoken distance, how far away must Jesus be? The distance between God and the world was an unspoken part of the landscape in which I lived. Belief in God was nearly universal, and yet that belief did little to shape daily life. There was a moral connection, a sense that our world was related to God through the things it "ought" to do, or through the things it "should" believe. But a great gulf was fixed between the dwelling place of God and the stage on which daily life occurred. Few things illustrated that gulf more clearly than the absence of those who had died.

The shape of the universe of my childhood was not the invention of Southern Protestantism. It was part of a much larger culture, forged in the crucible of the Protestant Reformation and the birth of the modern world in the sixteenth and seventeenth centuries. Today it is the dominant shape of the universe shared by most cultures of the modern Western world. It is the universe in which modern believers live. It is also a universe increasingly hostile to religious belief.

I have come to think of this modern cultural construct as the "two-storey universe." It is as though the universe were a two-storey house: We live here on earth, the first floor, where things are simply things and everything operates according to normal, natural laws, while God lives in heaven, upstairs, and is largely removed from the storey in which we live. To effect anything here, God must interrupt the laws of nature and perform a miracle. Exactly how often He does this is a matter of debate among Christians and many others within our culture—often measured by just how conservative or liberal their religion may be. The effects of this distance are all-encompassing in the area of religious experience and belief, and frequently in other areas as well.

I spent two years of my ministry serving as a hospice chaplain in East Tennessee. My work was in the homes of terminally ill patients—listening to them and their families, and offering whatever I could that would be of help at the end of life. The culture in those situations was largely the same as I had known as a child. However, I was now observing it as an adult. The ritual of death and dying had changed little, at least in rural areas. The shape of the universe was maintained. Though the belief was unspoken, most understood that we live in a two-storey universe. In the course of that ministry, it became clear to me that the distance between the first floor and the second—the perceived distance between daily life and God—created a great uncertainty about the dead and brought inherent complications to grief.

There is a dark side for religious belief in the context of the two-storey universe. The dark secret thought that is often avoided is the suspicion that no one lives on the second floor: neither God nor the dead. That which is normal and ordinary, all that we think of as the first floor, may be all there is. The dark side of the two-storey universe is that unbelief and atheism are its most natural expressions. The second floor is a religious construct that seeks to salvage something of the universe that predated the rise of secular thought. But in the context of a two-storey universe, such efforts will always be a losing battle.

The two-storey universe is another way of describing a secular culture. The word *secular* should never be confused with *atheist*. Instead it refers to a separation between our daily life and God. This separation had its foundation in the religious and political wars of the sixteenth and seventeenth centuries. The easiest way to achieve peace between warring religious factions was to remove religious debate from the sphere of daily living. At first this segregation was achieved by declaring separate religions for separate countries. The Peace of Augsburg (1555) offered the formula *cuius regio, eius religio*, establishing the principle that the religion of the ruling prince (*eius religio*) would be the religion of any given political area (*cuius regio*). This formula was successful where populations remained religiously homogeneous, although it involved the relocation of some populations in order to achieve that homogeneity.

However, the world refused to remain religiously homogeneous. At the same time that Europe was segregating itself along religious lines, the New World was reversing the trend. By the end of the eighteenth century, the United States came into existence as the first intentionally secular state. That the state was secular did not mean that it was unbelieving. Rather, there was no identifiable religion of the state: *eius religio* was exiled to the second storey. The state (*cuius regio*) was officially the first floor, with no particular religious loyalty or presence.

In the secular world, there are spheres which God may not enter—or if He does, He must remain quiet and unidentified. Most of these spheres are political and public. However, secular space, a sort of religious neutral zone, has a marked tendency to grow rather than to shrink. There are, of course, places where God may enter (such as churches), but even there the space is increasingly threatened by His presence. A growing number of "seeker-friendly" churches downplay the connection with God, preferring to offer "life-coaching." Some denominational parishes today have removed from their signs any reference to their denomination, sometimes failing even to mention that the sign is for a church. In my city, the local Unitarian-Universalist community insists on paying property taxes, acknowledging the state in a way that marks the triumph of the secular.

An odor of doubt surrounds all things religious within the first storey. This same doubt is sometimes stated frankly in a mild form of religious agnosticism ("no one can speak with certainty about God"), or in a desperate reaction which

> *Whenever God and all things associated with Him are exiled from daily life, it is a foregone conclusion that God and all things associated with Him will become increasingly irrelevant and foreign to the lives we live.*

gives birth to a raging fundamentalism that sees all things secular as the enemy. There is among many religious believers a profound sense that something has been lost—that the culture has slipped away and become a contradiction to believing. This sense of loss is not unjustified; but the loss began centuries ago.

Whenever God and all things associated with Him are exiled from daily life—whenever words such as "normal" and "ordinary" are used to describe the world without God—it is a foregone conclusion that

God and all things associated with Him will become increasingly irrelevant and foreign to the lives we live. A God who has been exiled to the second floor will soon seem no more than the story of a God, and finally no God at all.

This odor of doubt surrounding most things religious in our culture creates a market for miracles, stories of near-death experiences ("there-and-back-again"), and an undue interest in paranormal phenomena. A friend of mine, a monk from Belarus, once tellingly commented, "You Americans! You talk about miracles like you don't believe in God!" The doubt of the first-floor Christian is not quite the same thing as unbelief, but it is a powerful reflection of the distance at which God sits. Any news of footsteps on the second floor, or of someone "visiting" from upstairs, gathers attention among the first-floor dwellers. The thought is that if anything reaches us from the second floor, there might be a God after all.

In this divided universe, prayer is problematic. Why do we pray, and are our prayers heard? To pray about things in the secular world—the world of the first floor—is to ask God to intervene in the nature of things, to set aside the very laws of the universe. It is sometimes said on a popular level that a prayer "didn't get beyond the ceiling." That may indeed be a legitimate concern in a universe constructed with two stories.

The two-storey universe also has consequences for the world in which we live. If the earth is a neutral zone, then our relationship with the things within it carries no particular religious or moral weight. This consequence has led many environmental activists to blame Christianity itself for the abuse of the ecosphere. It is a gross overstatement to say that Christianity is to blame for the world's environmental problems. The dynamics of our modern civilization and its industrial life are far too complex to be explained in such a manner. It is true, on the other hand, that all is not well between tree and Church. A world from which God is exiled is a world where nothing is sacred. The consequences of such an absence cannot help but be disastrous.

The two-storey universe has many far more subtle effects. The very character of our relationship with God in such a universe is reduced to the moral or forensic level. God is not with us; He is absent from us. Our life is not united to His life; it is a life understood to be as secularized and independent as the world in which it dwells. Christianity can call its adherents to be good, but such goodness will itself be little more than a variation of secular goodness. At the same time, morality quickly becomes political morality, for politics is the defining characteristic of a world understood as separated from God.

Just as religious belief is encumbered with an ever-present doubt in a two-storey universe, so everything of the first floor tends to collapse in on itself as God is removed. Dostoevsky is popularly quoted as having said, "Without God, everything is permitted." But where everything is permitted, the value of any one thing is diminished. The removal of God from daily life leaves little more than raw power (or wealth) as the arbiter of all things. G. K. Chesterton once wrote, "When a man ceases to believe in God, it is not so much that he believes in nothing, as it is that he is willing to believe in anything." Beauty is strained in a world devoid of God. To what does Beauty refer if God is not present?

With the universe divided and its secularly conceived component dominating our daily life, the transcendent begins to elude us, and the world begins to drown in a sea of literalism. In the ultimate banality of the secular world, "what you see is what you get." Time becomes chronology, and history triumphs over all. True eschatology, the moment-by-moment in-breaking of the Kingdom of God, ceases to have a place within the Christian world. Scripture becomes lost in a constant battle between opposing camps of literalists—those who believe literal history negates the Bible and those who believe the Bible *is* literal history.

This bifurcated universe is not the legacy of Christianity but a deviation from its legacy. The accidents of politics and philosophy have reduced our understanding and experience of human existence. But such sad turns in human history are not the final word. The witness to a deeper Christianity and a world in which God is "everywhere present and filling all things" has not disappeared. This book is an effort to draw back the curtain and look at both the emptiness of our present understanding and the fullness of our Christian inheritance.

It should be noted in this first chapter that the imagery of a two-storey world is not original with me. I first encountered a version of the image in the writings of the Protestant thinker Francis Schaeffer. He used it to describe a division in the nature of truth. My use of the image is far more mundane, though I must acknowledge where it first appeared to me. By the same token, looking at the nature of the world conceived in a secular manner has been a not uncommon late-twentieth-century observation. Fr. Alexander Schmemann had much to say on the topic in his wonderful little book, *For the Life of the World*. The Roman Catholic writer Thomas Howard did something of the same thing in his book, *Splendor in the Ordinary*.

It would seem to me that anyone who comes from a sacramental tradition should feel a certain cognitive dissonance with the sounds and images of secularized thought. For the God who took flesh and dwelt among us is surely the same God who continues to take common things like bread and wine, oil and water, as well as men and women, and make of them the instruments of His presence among us. For He is indeed everywhere present and filling all things.

CHAPTER TWO

SITTING IN A CAVE IN MAR SABA

Mar Saba (the Monastery of St. Sabbas the Sanctified) is one of the oldest continuously functioning Orthodox monasteries in the world. It is situated in the Judean desert outside of Jerusalem, clinging to cliffs overlooking the Kidron Valley. There are no trees, nothing to ease the sun's intensity. But there are caves. On one side of the ravine is a structure that today serves the fifteen monks who live there. The structure houses a number of important things—such as the refectory, where the community eats—but behind the façade of the monastery is a warren of caves and passageways carved into the rock of the cliff. These caves have served as the dwellings of monastics for well over a millennium and a half.

I had come to Mar Saba as part of a larger pilgrimage to the Holy Land. My interest in Mar Saba was in looking for one particular cave—the cell of St. John of Damascus. St. John came to the monastery after leaving the court of the Muslim caliph. It was in this cave that he wrote his most famous works: *On the Holy Icons* and *The Exact Exposition of the Orthodox Faith*.

Sitting in the cave (which is about ten feet by eight feet by my guesstimate), it is hard to imagine praying, much less producing theological works of lasting value. A ledge served as St. John's bed. A small niche held his icons and lampada, and another convenient niche held a desk.

EVERYWHERE PRESENT

Seeing his surroundings, it is hard to fathom that this monastery was once one of the great library centers of the Church and the origin of the Typicon of St. Saba, still the dominant Typicon (book of directions for all services) used in the Orthodox Church. Mar Saba is not only an old monastery, but among the most important in the history of Orthodox Christianity.

I was sitting in St. John's cave, thinking of all these things and trying to pray. My prayers were for the intercessions of St. John. I write—and no one wrote better or more clearly on the Orthodox faith than St. John of Damascus. What I found in the monastery was much more than a cramped cave: I found an outpost of the one-storey universe.

The monks at Mar Saba are not from another century. However, their way of life, formed and shaped by the monastic Typicon that originated there, has baptized them into a way of seeing and perceiving the world around them that has largely been lost to the modern West. You know immediately that you are in a different place when you enter the *catholicon*, the central church that serves the monks. The catholicon itself was first discovered by St. Saba. His own cave/cell was originally on the other side of the ravine. One night he saw a light shining upwards from the opposite cliff. When he investigated, he found a sizable cave that was oriented in the proper direction (eastward) and shaped like the inside of a church. There was even an outcropping of rock where an altar should be. The cave, the rock—all became the catholicon ("revealed by God," in the words of St. Saba).

Icons mounted on the walls within the usual configuration of a Byzantine chapel are the first sights that visitors see upon entering the catholicon. However, after a first glance, it is impossible to overlook a transept, opposite the entrance, that is lined with skulls. This monastic chapel clearly presents a different view of death from the one I knew in my childhood. Here you not only speak of death—it stares you in the face and speaks for itself. The skulls are those of martyred monks. There have been many through the centuries, all dying at the hands of various invading armies or surrounding groups who hated them for their religion, or mistakenly believed the monastery to hold treasure. It does hold treasure, but not the sort imagined by the makers of martyrs.

The monk who was serving as our guide was asked by a pilgrim if the monastery had difficulties with its Muslim and Jewish neighbors. "The monastery has been here for a long time. We have had many different neighbors," he answered. Then he added, "But we are monks. We have no enemies."

I had found paradise.

I also found interesting stories. At the time of my visit, one of the brotherhood had "fallen asleep" some two weeks earlier. "We never say that a monk has died," our guide told us, and I suddenly imagined the unspokenness of death that I knew so well. He continued, "We always say, in the words of Scripture, that they have 'fallen asleep.' But mostly we say this because we see them so often."

Now I knew I was in a different place.

"You see them?" I asked.

"Sure," he said. "They appear to the monks all the time. It's nothing to see St. Saba on the stairs or elsewhere." The witness of the monk (who happened to be from San Francisco) was not a tale of the unexpected. These were not ghostly visits he was describing, but the living presence of the saints who inhabit the same space as ourselves. It is a one-storey universe. Such stories from the monastery of Mar Saba could be duplicated all over the Orthodox monastic world. That which separates the monks of the present from the fathers of the past is very thin indeed. It is not only a one-storey universe, but a fairly crowded universe, at that.

The doctrine of the ancient Church is quite clear in this matter.

EVERYWHERE PRESENT

Those who have died are separated from us in the body—but the Church remains One. There is not one Church on earth and another in heaven. There is one Church, of which all Orthodox believers are members. Nothing seemed more natural to these monks than the presence, occasionally visible, of the monks of Mar Saba, regardless of the century in which they dwelt there in the body. The monks of Mar Saba are all there—in the hands of God.

Such an understanding is only possible where the distance between God and man, between heaven and earth, has been overcome. The doctrine of the Incarnation teaches us that God has become man and dwelt among us. In the God-man Christ Jesus, heaven and earth are united, and the distance between God and man, of whatever sort, is overcome.

Nothing seemed more natural to these monks than the presence, occasionally visible, of the monks of Mar Saba, regardless of the century in which they dwelt there in the body.

It is interesting that the Gospels of Matthew, Mark, Luke, and John all make clear that the disciples of Christ were not quite prepared for this union of heaven and earth. Despite living 1500 years before the modern construction of the two-storey universe, they seem to have lived in an ancient version of their own. The Jews certainly held a belief that God worked in history, but the marriage of heaven and earth was more than they expected—even from a messiah. Thus when Christ appears to His disciples on the shore of the Sea of Galilee, he asks them for something to eat. It is proof to them that in His resurrection He is not a ghost. The resurrection of Christ is not an example of life after death, but of the destruction of death itself: "Christ is risen from the dead, / trampling down death by death, / and upon those in the tombs bestowing life."

This is the Church's hymn of Pascha, celebrating the resurrection of Christ. It does not sing that Christ has died and gone to heaven to be with His Father. Though the story of the ascension of Christ into heaven does speak of His being seated at the right hand of the Father, the stories of the resurrection make it quite clear that the Christ who sits at the right hand of the Father is no ghostly spirit, but the risen Lord, who has carried earth and man to the right hand of the Almighty. It is not a two-storey account, but the very basis for belief in a one-storey universe.

The theological term for this doctrine of the Church is the *communion of the saints*. It would be accurate to say that the Church's teaching is the communion of everything, for the very heart of the ancient Christian faith is the belief that our salvation itself is a communion with God. We live because we have communion with God, and only because we have communion with Him. "Then Jesus said to them, 'Most assuredly, I say to you, unless you eat the flesh of the Son of Man and drink His blood, you have no life in you'" (John 6:53).

We have life in ourselves—we truly live—only because the Life of God has been given to us in Holy Baptism, and nourished in the Holy Sacraments and in our daily communion with God in all things. Our salvation is not an external matter in which we receive permission from God to spend eternity in a special place called heaven. Though this imagery is popular (particularly in Hollywood), it is simply not the Gospel as taught in the New Testament and given as Living Tradition in the Church. The arena in which we work out our salvation is nothing other than the world in which we live—which is permeated and sustained by the presence of God, and where we ourselves are "surrounded by so great a cloud of witnesses" (Hebrews 12:1). The monks of Mar Saba, like so many others, bear witness to this wondrous cloud and to the union of heaven and earth.

The experience of these dear monks differs strikingly from that of most who dwell in the two-storey universe of modern Christianity. I

17

recall a question put to me some years ago by a young Baptist widow. I was serving as a hospice chaplain at the time. When her young husband died, her question was, "Will he be aware of me when he goes to heaven?" To a degree, her question and her anxiety were driven by a two-storey vision of the universe. Her departed husband was going to live "up there." Would he know what was happening in her life "down here"?

The perceived gap (a purely theological construct) places her husband in a position where he is potentially unaware of our life. The Scriptures, however, teach us something quite different. The "great cloud of witnesses" is, in fact, the great company of heaven—the departed who are in the "hands of God." Their concerns are not separated from ours, for they are not separated from the Body of Christ.

> The Body of Christ is one Body. There is only One Church—not divided between those who have fallen asleep in Christ and those who remain behind.

If you read the Revelation of St. John, it becomes clear that the primary concern of the inhabitants of heaven, within the great saint's vision, is with matters on earth. There is a battle here on earth, and there is a war there in heaven. The "place of verdure, a place of rest" found in the Church's prayers (particularly for the departed) is, according to Holy Scripture, not a place oblivious to our own turmoil. I suspect that the descriptions in our prayers for the departed are eschatological visions of what will be when the battle is over and the strife is past. But it is quite clear that Scripture has no notion of a two-storey world in which some of us are struggling for the salvation of our souls, while the rest can wipe their brows and say, "I'm glad that's over."

The Body of Christ is one Body. There is only One Church—not divided between those who have fallen asleep in Christ and those who remain behind. Whether we are here or in the hand of God, the struggle is the struggle of the whole Church. My success or failure in my spiritual life is not my private business, but the concern of a great cloud of witnesses. Neither are they watching only as disinterested bystanders. They urge us on and support us with their prayers. Were they to watch us without participating at the same time in our struggles, the watching would be like torture. As it is, their watching is prayer and participation of the deepest sort.

It is for this reason (among many) that many services in the Eastern Church contain the phrase, "Lord, Jesus Christ, through the prayers of our holy fathers, have mercy on us and save us." It is a humility of sorts, a demurring to the prayers of greater Christians—but it is also calling on a reality that abides. We are not alone. The great cloud of witnesses stands with me and in me in prayer.

Every prayer we ourselves offer is a participation in the life of the world. We have a participation in the great cloud of witnesses, but we also have a participation in everyone who is. The prayer of a righteous few has an amazing salvific impact on the life of the world. If they'd had but a few more righteous men, Sodom and Gomorrah would still be standing. To this day we do not know how many or how few, in their righteous prayers, preserve us before God.

I can recall a conversation with one of my brothers some years back. He wondered about the hermits in the desert. He had an admiration for the asceticism of their lifestyle. His question, however, was, "But what is the value when no one knows they are there?" The truth is that God knows they are there. The devil knows they are there, and he trembles. And we all know they are there, whether it is a conscious knowing or not. For their prayers permeate us, and our prayers join with theirs as they rise before God.

Among the most fundamental understandings of the New

Testament is the reality and promise of communion (Greek *koinonia*). It means a commonality, a sharing and a participation in the same thing. This koinonia lies at the very heart of the New Testament's understanding of salvation. It lies equally at the heart of the understanding of prayer. The life of the monks of Mar Saba, their experience of a common life with even the departed monks of their community, is a manifestation of this koinonia. The loss of communion as a theological foundation is a large part of the false construction of the two-storey universe, as well as of modernity's alienation from God.

Communion is a central part of Jesus' teaching about His relationship with humanity. In one of His primary images, He portrays Himself as a vine with us as branches:

"I am the true vine, and My Father is the vinedresser. Every branch in Me that does not bear fruit He takes away; and every *branch* that bears fruit He prunes, that it may bear more fruit. You are already clean because of the word which I have spoken to you. Abide in Me, and I in you. As the branch cannot bear fruit of itself, unless it abides in the vine, neither can you, unless you abide in Me. I am the vine, you *are* the branches. He who abides in Me, and I in him, bears much fruit; for without Me you can do nothing. If anyone does not abide in Me, he is cast out as a branch and is withered; and they gather them and throw *them* into the fire, and they are burned. If you abide in Me, and My words abide in you, you will ask what you desire, and it shall be done for you. By this My Father is glorified, that you bear much fruit; so you will be My disciples." (John 15:1–8)

To abide in Christ as a branch abides in a vine is to live a life of communion—the life of the vine is the life of the branches. The branches do not lie on the ground and talk about a wonderful vine that lives somewhere else. Branch and vine form one existence.

This communion is also described in Christ's "high priestly prayer":

> "I do not pray for these alone, but also for those who will believe in Me through their word; that they all may be one, as You, Father, *are* in Me, and I in You; that they also may be one in Us, that the world may believe that You sent Me. And the glory which You gave Me I have given them, that they may be one just as We are one: I in them, and You in Me; that they may be made perfect in one, and that the world may know that You have sent Me, and have loved them as You have loved Me." (John 17:20–23)

The unity for which Christ prays is no mere *quality* of our life in Christ; it *is* our life in Christ. That this unity (communion) is the very life of salvation is made clear in St. John's first epistle:

> This is the message which we have heard from Him and declare to you, that God is light and in Him is no darkness at all. If we say that we have fellowship [*koinonia*] with Him, and walk in darkness, we lie and do not practice the truth. But if we walk in the light as He is in the light, we have fellowship [*koinonia*] with one another, and the blood of Jesus Christ His Son cleanses us from all sin. (1 John 1:5–7)

27

Here our communion with God is described as a *communion of light*—though the nature of that light is made clear: God is light. St. John uses the image of light to say that our communion is a true participation in God, in His very life.

This same saving participation in the life of God is presented in Christ's discourse on the Eucharist:

> Then Jesus said to them, "Most assuredly, I say to you,
> unless you eat the flesh of the Son of Man and drink
> His blood, you have no life in you. Whoever eats
> My flesh and drinks My blood has eternal life, and I
> will raise him up at the last day. For My flesh is food
> indeed, and My blood is drink indeed. He who eats My
> flesh and drinks My blood abides in Me, and I in him.
> As the living Father sent Me, and I live because of the
> Father, so he who feeds on Me will live because of Me."
> (John 6:53–57)

Many English translations of the Scripture render *koinonia* as "fellowship." In older English usage, this rendering may not have been problematic. However, in modern English, such a translation is simply a travesty. It trivializes our life in Christ—using (unwittingly, I hope) a noun that today merely describes a church social event. Christ has not come into the world in order to share a cup of coffee. This shift in the meaning and rendering of words is itself a testimony to the change that has happened to the context of our language over time. Fellowship as conviviality (itself a corruption of its original meaning) rather than "common life" is a demonstration of the isolation that has crept into the modern understanding of human existence. We are today seen as discrete, individual existences whose life is self-defined. We may share common interests and common moments with others, but our life is our own. This is a contradiction of the assumptions contained within koinonia.

The communion of saints is a fundamental doctrine of the Christian faith. The Apostles' Creed, recited in many Western churches, makes reference to the communion of saints as an article of faith. Its place within the Apostles' Creed, in addition to the Scriptures that teach it, is a testimony to its apostolic antiquity. There is no early Christian faith that does not have the communion of saints as a foundational understanding.

One of the best ways to begin thinking about communion with God is to ask the question, "What is wrong with the human race?" What is it about us that needs saving?

The answer to that question is perhaps the linchpin of Christian theology (at least of what has been revealed to us). Among the most central of Orthodox Christian doctrines is the understanding that human beings have fallen out of communion with God—we have severed the bond of communion with which we were created, and thus we are no longer in communion with the Lord and Giver of Life. We no longer have a share in His Divine Life, but instead have become partakers of death.

St. Athanasius describes this in his *On the Incarnation of the Word*:

> For God had made man thus (that is, as an embodied spirit), and had willed that he should remain in incorruption. But men, having turned from the contemplation of God to evil of their own devising, had come inevitably under the law of death. Instead of remaining in the state in which God had created them, they were in process of becoming corrupted entirely, and death had them completely under its dominion. For the transgression of the commandment

was making them turn back again according to their nature; and as they had at the beginning come into being out of non-existence, so were they now on the way to returning, through corruption, to non-existence again. The presence and love of the Word had called them into being; inevitably, therefore, when they lost the knowledge of God, they lost existence with it; for it is God alone Who exists, evil is non-being, the negation and antithesis of good. By nature, of course, man is mortal, since he was made from nothing; but he bears also the Likeness of Him Who is, and if he preserves that Likeness through constant contemplation, then his nature is deprived of its power and he remains incorrupt. So is it affirmed in Wisdom: "The keeping of His laws is the assurance of incorruption." (Wisdom 6.18)

This lack of communion with God, this process of death at work in us, manifests itself in a myriad of ways, extending from moral failure to disease and death itself. It corrupts everything around us—our relationships with other people, our institutions, and our best intentions.

Without intervention, the process of death results in the most final form of death—complete alienation and enmity with God (from our point of view). We come to hate all things righteous and good. We despise the Light and prefer darkness. Since this is the state of human beings who have cut themselves off from communion with God, we substitute many things and create a false life, mistaking wealth, fame, youth, sex, emotions, and so forth for true life.

Seeing all of this as true of humanity, the Orthodox Christian faith does not generally view humanity as having a legal or juridical problem.

It is not that we did something wrong and now owe a debt we cannot pay, or are being punished with death—though such a metaphor can be used and has its usefulness. But we need more than a change in our legal status; we need a change in our ontological status—that is, we must be filled with nothing less than the Life of God in order to be healed, forgiven, and made new. Jesus did not come to make bad men good; He came to make dead men live.

Thus God came into our world, becoming one of us, so that by His sharing in our life, we might have a share in His life. In Holy Baptism we are united to Him, and everything else He gives us in the Life of His Church is for the purpose of strengthening, nurturing, and renewing this Life within us. All the sacraments have this as their focus. It is the primary purpose of prayer.

Jesus did not come to make bad men good; He came to make dead men live.

Thus, stated simply, to have communion with God means to have a share in His Divine Life. He lives in me and I in Him. I come to know God even as I know myself. I come to love even as God loves, because it is His love that dwells in me. I come to forgive as God forgives, because it His mercy that dwells within me.

Without such an understanding of communion, many vitally important parts of the Christian life are reduced to mere moralisms. We are told to love our enemies as though it were a simple moral obligation. Instead, we love our enemies because God loves our enemies, and we want to live in the Life of God. We're not trying to be good, or to prove anything to God by loving our enemies. It is simply the case that if the Love of God dwells in us, then we will love as God loves.

Of course all this is the free gift of God, though living daily in communion with God is difficult. The disease of broken communion that was so long at work in us is difficult to cure. It takes time, and we must be patient with ourselves and our broken humanity—though never using this as an excuse not to seek the healing that God gives.

We were created for communion with God—it is our very life. Thinking about communion with God is not a substitute for that communion. Theology as abstraction has no life within it. Theology is a life lived in Christ. The ancient Christian writer Evagrius Ponticus famously said, "A theologian is one who prays, and one who prays is a theologian."

This lived communion, our true participation in the life of God and in the life of the world and of others, is the very shape of our salvation and the true nature of our existence. Life in a one-storey universe is what salvation looks like.

CHAPTER THREE

WE LIVE IN AN ALTAR

Children have a marvelous way of revealing things. Some time back, a young child in my parish clearly developed an attachment to me. It is never quite clear what such attachments mean—though at her age it generally means a fascination with God and even a confusion between who the priest is and who God is. On one Sunday, illness kept me away from the Sunday liturgy. My second priest took charge of the service. Throughout the service (we learned later) the child kept looking for me. As this door and that door would open, she would strain to see me. When, at the end of the service, it was clear that I was not there, she burst into tears. "Where is Father Stephen?"

Some weeks later, after a less stressful Sunday liturgy, this same child came to me and pointed into the altar: "That is where you live," she said. My first reaction was to want to say, "No. I live in a house down the street." But a very deep part of me could not bring myself to say that I do not live in the altar. It is certainly wrong to say I merely work in the altar. My relationship with this child and her childlike perceptions forced me to rethink where I live.

It is not an insignificant question: "Where do you live?" On the level of our relationship with God, it is far more than a mere question of where a GPS would locate your domicile. By the same token, it is a very serious question to ask, "Where does God live?" And to answer, "He is everywhere present," is simply not sufficient. For to live everywhere could be tantamount to living nowhere. If it is true that God is everywhere, then we must think and speak carefully about *how* God is everywhere present, and not simply assume that the answer of "everywhere" is any answer at all. *How* is frequently more important than *where*.

It is not unusual for a child to ask, "Where is heaven?" Many adults may wonder the same thing but rarely speak it. When the question is put in such blatant, literal terms, most people realize that it is insufficient to say heaven is "up there." The famous quote attributed to Yuri Gagarin, the first man in space, that while in orbit he did not see God, only points to the quasi-humorous character of literal statements about heaven. Heaven is not literally "up there." But if this is true, then where is heaven? Where does God live?

On the one hand, we may say that "God dwells in heaven." But the Church also says that He is "everywhere present and filling all things." It is not incorrect to conclude from these two statements that "heaven is everywhere." Again, this is an answer that is so generally true that it is of little particular use. Traditional Christian language, when referring to God, heaven, and the like, often has a strange character. As we go further, we will see more of how God is present, and in that way perhaps see both our world and heaven more clearly, as well as gaining an ear for the Church's language.

The odd character of traditional Christian language became quite clear to me during a pilgrimage to Israel. We visited most of the traditional sites and enjoyed many blessings. We sailed on the Sea of Galilee and received communion in the Church of the Holy Sepulchre. We made a pilgrimage to the Jordan River. It was during our visit to the Jordan River that this strange quality of Christian language became obvious.

We gathered at the water's edge and stood in silence as the bishop leading our pilgrimage intoned the words for the great blessing of the waters.

"Great art Thou, O Lord, and marvelous are Thy works! No word is sufficient to hymn Thy praises!" the bishop chanted. As the prayer continued, the now-familiar words of the prayer created a sort of cognitive dissonance: "That the Lord our God will send down the blessing of Jordan, and sanctify these waters, let us pray to the Lord . . ." What does it mean for God to "send down the blessing of Jordan" on the waters of the Jordan themselves?

Fr. Alexander Schmemann famously made the point that sacraments do not make things to be something they are not—they reveal things to be what they truly are.[1] This was surely the case in the blessing of the Jordan River. For God to send down the "blessing of Jordan" on the Jordan River itself can only be to reveal the river to be what it already is.

But this becomes the key question: "What is the Jordan River?" It is similar to the question, "Where is God?" On a literal level, the Jordan River cannot be made more the Jordan River than it already is. If God is everywhere present, then on a literal level He cannot be made more present than He already is.

This is the failure of literalism. It is certainly possible to walk beside the Jordan River and have no idea of where you are. As rivers go, it is just one more stream of water. Angels do not sing as you approach, nor do the waters automatically part when you seek to cross it. The

1 *For the Life of the World*, St. Vladimir's Seminary Press, 1973, pp. 131–132

presence of God everywhere is not accompanied by trumpets or Hollywood's special effects. The lack of such unusual qualities often leads modern men and women to see nothing more than the obvious. It is possible to tour the Sistine Chapel and describe Michelangelo's ceiling as "a collection of colors." Such a description, however, could easily evoke the response, "Then you never visited the Sistine Chapel."

For some the "problem" of many things carrying a double meaning is resolved by placing one of the meanings within the mind of the person who sees it. Thus, something is literally one thing, while a person may understand it to be another. The Sistine Chapel is literally marked by a collection of colors, but is understood as beautiful and a work of genius by an educated witness. Of course, this distinction has the handicap of saying that things are really only their material components—anything more is in the eye (or mind) of the beholder. Thus the significance of reality is somehow less than real—it becomes merely psychological or cultural. This is another manifestation of the two-storey universe. The first floor on which we all live is "real," while the second floor is found "in the understanding" of some. In time, this understanding is more and more challenged. That which is understood to be the "true" reality eventually becomes the only reality. The second floor is the least stable of all imagined places.

Christian tradition, in its oldest form, has always offered a different, more unified account of reality. This account can primarily be found in the Church's teaching on the sacraments or mysteries (as the sacraments are called in Eastern tradition).

> Then Jesus said to them, "Most assuredly, I say to you,
> unless you eat the flesh of the Son of Man and drink
> His blood, you have no life in you. Whoever eats
> My flesh and drinks My blood has eternal life, and I

will raise him up at the last day. For My flesh is food indeed, and My blood is drink indeed. He who eats My flesh and drinks My blood abides in Me, and I in him. As the living Father sent Me, and I live because of the Father, so he who feeds on Me will live because of Me. This is the bread which came down from heaven—not as your fathers ate the manna, and are dead. He who eats this bread will live forever." (John 6:53–58)

In St. John's Gospel, Christ's discourse on the Holy Eucharist takes place following the miracle of the feeding of the five thousand. St. John introduces for the first time language that will become the common language of the Church. The bread and the wine Christ gives His disciples at the Last Supper are introduced with the words:

And He took bread, gave thanks and broke *it,* and gave *it* to them, saying, "This is My body which is given for you; do this in remembrance of Me." Likewise He also *took* the cup after supper, saying, "This cup *is* the new covenant in My blood, which is shed for you." (Luke 22:19–20)

The consistent agreement of the early Church was to treat these words as descriptions of reality. There were no theories explaining the words "body" and "blood" as symbolic or somehow less than true. They were not mental concepts about the bread and wine, but words that truly and accurately describe what is given in the Eucharist.

Writing in the third century, St. Irenaeus, Bishop of Lyons, offered this intriguing statement: "Our teaching agrees with the Eucharist and the Eucharist confirms our teaching" (*Against the Heresies*, 4.18.5). In the passage in which this statement occurs, St. Irenaeus was arguing for the very heart of the Christian understanding of the world. God makes Himself present to us through the very things of this world. In St. Irenaeus's language, "There are two realities."

In a variety of ways, the early Church bore witness to life in a one-storey world in which God is truly "everywhere present."

In a variety of ways, the early Church would maintain this worldview. The sacraments were not psychological events but truly the very things we called them. Centuries later, icons would be defended as truly making present what they represent in color. Scripture was seen as having many layers of meaning and encompassing far more than its most immediate literal sense. The world was not simple matter—devoid of any meaning other than that inferred through ideas. The world was not a two-storey universe with an empty, meaningless collection of matter in which humanity lives and a lofty, removed paradise of heaven where all things divine dwell. In a variety of ways, the early Church bore witness to life in a one-storey world in which God is truly "everywhere present."

In all of these things, the Church bore a faithful and consistent witness to the very character of the world created by God. We do not live in a world of mere things, disconnected and without reference to one another and to God. Creation exists with the capacity to reveal God: "For since the creation of the world His invisible *attributes* are clearly seen, being understood by the things that are made, *even* His eternal power and Godhead" (Romans 1:20).

None of this denies the material character of creation. Rather, the material world is declared by the life of the Church to be a holy place, a place whose true character is revealed only in reference to God. The mysteries of the Church do not destroy matter or make it cease to be material. Even in the great mystery of the Holy Eucharist, the bread is not destroyed:

> For we offer to Him His own, announcing consistently the fellowship and union of the flesh and Spirit. For as the bread, which is produced from the earth, when it receives the invocation of God, is no longer common bread, but the Eucharist, consisting of two realities, earthly and heavenly; so also our bodies, when they receive the Eucharist, are no longer corruptible, having the hope of the resurrection to eternity. (Irenaeus, *Against the Heresies,* 4.18.5)

The "two realities" are not separate but one, given to us in a mystery. I do not mean to offer any theory of consecration in quoting St. Irenaeus, nor is he suggesting one. Concern for the spiritual mechanics of the sacraments is a fairly late development in the Christian faith. Irenaeus's own statement is that the bread is no longer "common bread" but is the "Eucharist."

In the mystery of Holy Baptism, the priest does not pray for the water to become something other than water. He does indeed pray for the "blessing of Jordan" to come down on the waters (just as we prayed for the blessing of Jordan to come down on the waters of the Jordan itself). These great mysteries of the Church unite us with God, but they do not unite us in a manner that ignores the creation through which this union occurs. Creation is not made to be other than creation. The truth of creation and its relationship to man and God are revealed to be what they truly are: the communion of heaven and earth.

St. John of Damascus, writing in the eighth century, offers a strong statement of the interrelationship between the material world and our salvation:

> Of old, God the incorporeal and uncircumscribed was never depicted. Now, however, when God is seen clothed in flesh, and conversing with men, I make an image of the God whom I see. I do not worship matter; I worship the God of matter, who became matter for my sake, and deigned to inhabit matter, who worked out my salvation through matter. I will not cease from honoring that matter which works my salvation. I venerate it, though not as God. How could God be born out of lifeless things?
>
> . . . I honor all matter besides, and venerate it. Through it, filled, as it were, with a divine power and grace, my salvation has come to me. Was not the thrice-happy and thrice-blessed wood of the Cross matter? Was not the sacred and holy mountain of Calvary matter? What of the life-giving rock, the Holy Sepulcher, the source of our resurrection: was it not matter? Is not the most holy book of the Gospels matter? Is not the blessed table matter which gives us the Bread of Life? Are not the gold and silver matter, out of which crosses and altar-plate and chalices are made? And before all these things, is not the body and blood of our Lord matter? Either do away with the veneration and worship due to all these things, or submit to the tradition of the Church in the veneration of images,

honoring God and His friends, and following in this
the grace of the Holy Spirit. Do not despise matter,
for it is not despicable. (*In Defense of the Holy
Images,* 1.15–17)

My child friend was correct in saying, "You live in the altar," though
she said far more than she knew. The material world is declared by
the life of the Church to be a holy place, a place whose true character
is revealed only in reference to God. "The whole earth is full of His
glory," is the testimony sung before God by the angels (Isaiah 6:3). We
do not live in a world of *mere* matter. We live in a world filled with
holy matter. We live in an altar.

CHAPTER FOUR

THE GOD
WHO IS
NOT THERE

One of the hallmarks of the two-storey universe is its difficulty with the presence of God. The problem extends beyond the theological question of "where is God?" and becomes a problem with all things religious. The culture of the two-storey universe communicates to its inhabitants the distinct feeling that something is out of place when religious artifacts appear outside of a church (and for some, even when they appear inside).

As an Orthodox priest, I follow the tradition of wearing my cassock in public. For years prior to being Orthodox, as an Anglican priest, I wore a clerical collar in public. Thus, for the past thirty years or so I have been publicly identified as a "religious object." Any priest or cleric who dresses contrary to secular fashion can testify to the experience of "invading public space." I have, on occasion, been accosted on the street by angry people, some of whom cannot bear the sight of something religious in public. Others want to engage in religious debate, feeling challenged by a mode of dress that publicly signals a religious position other than their own.

Despite such experiences, most believers would say that they want to know the presence of God. His absence—particularly as a by-product of a secularized world—is a problem.

Interestingly, God's absence is not always a problem for everyone. A friend of mine some years back, a woman of the Old South, attended a renewal weekend sponsored by her church. She came home, and like others who had attended, evidenced a clear religious experience. Something had happened in her weekend renewal. However, to my surprise, after about a week of this new experience, she commented to me, "I just can't take it anymore! Jesus just seems to be everywhere! I can't get any work done!"

She continued, "So, I finally told Him, 'Jesus, please leave my kitchen and get back on Your throne! I can't get my cooking done!'" Apparently cooking takes place on the first floor—while Jesus reigns on the second.

Tragedy reminds us of God's apparent absence, but our cries of abandonment seem empty in light of the demands we make for God's absence at most other times and places.

The absence of God, in a two-storey arrangement, is not so noticeable for a secularized mind. Nothing seems to be out of place. Our world functions according to its laws, and we get by as best we can. Of course, plenty of prayers are uttered for winning lottery combinations and other selfish concerns, but these seem to have little bearing on the problem of God's absence. It is another story, however, when great tragedy strikes. In the wake of the tsunami that swept through the Indian Ocean in 2007, major newspapers in America (and elsewhere) asked the question, "Where is God?" Tragedy reminds us of God's apparent absence, but our cries of abandonment seem empty in light of the demands we make for God's absence at most other times and places.

The absence of God attached to the culture of the two-storey universe should not be confused with the classic experience of the "absence of God" found in the lives of many saints. In those cases, the absence has deep significance because the presence of God and intimate communion is sought above all else: God's presence is recognized as the source and gift of all life. But the absence established by our culture is an effort to regulate the presence of God: now we want Him, now we don't.

Such a desire for God's absence has not always been part of the culture of the Western world. Indeed, its evolution within Western societies seems to have begun unintentionally. As moderns, we live in a world that is the result of a massive operation of the law of unintended consequences. For instance, it is possible to eliminate holy days under the slogan, "All days are holy" (a common sentiment among many early Protestant groups). It is, of course, true that all days are holy. However, not long after all days are declared holy—and therefore no particular day is singled out as holy—the result will be that no day is holy. The same can be said for the abolition of the traditional priesthood. If the priesthood of all believers is the only form in which believers encounter the priesthood, before long there will be no encounter with the priesthood whatsoever.

A deeper principle is at work in all this than the law of unintended consequences, a principle that creates the consequences with which we now live. That principle is simply this: We do not know or experience anything in *general*—only in *particular*. We may have an abstract notion in our mind, but we cannot truly give it expression unless we do so in a particular manner. "All days are holy" is an abstraction. It may even be a true abstraction. But unless some particular days are holy in a unique way, then the statement "all days are holy" will have no meaning. The very word "definition" means to give something a boundary. Without boundaries, we have no idea what we are seeing or what is being shown to us. For a variety of ideological, theological, and political reasons, boundaries that had once existed in Christian civilization were abolished. The result was not the freedom of Christian civilization, but its disappearance. Something new had taken its place: the world of God's absence.

This world of absence is not the same thing as a world that is hostile to God (though our world often is). No one at the time of the Reformation was interested in abolishing religion; that would wait until later, more dangerous revolutions. The abolition of boundaries—of particular expressions of the presence of God—required the removal of what had once been Christian civilization. Within history, this often meant the abolition of particular holy days, the abolition of the apostolic priesthood, the destruction of religious images, and the erection of ever-growing walls between religious life and public life. In time the sacraments within the Church itself would be largely secularized, referencing a reality that was often "absent" in any manner other than the strictly ideal.

A God who is exiled from the mundane is understandably difficult to find when the mundane turns into the tragic.

The most convenient way to deconstruct these boundaries and create this absence was not to attack God Himself (or religion, *per se*), but to move them to a second storey, an "upstairs" of the universe of our experience. There God (in abstraction) and all matters religious (again in abstraction) could be placed until needed. The difficulty, of course, is that having once been exiled, such things do not necessarily return when needed. A God who is exiled from the mundane is understandably difficult to find when the mundane turns into the tragic.

The modern response by Christians to the crisis of God's absence has frequently been less than successful. Christians living within a secularized world often find the means provided by the secular order to be the only answer to the questions of culture. Thus, for many the legislation of God's presence seems the only course of action. Those who are comfortable with the world of God's absence are understandably nervous about such efforts—and in the final analysis, the problem of the presence of God is not something that can be addressed in the world of political action.

The greater problem is a world in which the absence of God is an actual construct of human understanding. Such constructs not only govern a culture's perception of the presence of God, but render the personal encounter with the presence of God problematic as well. Just as making every day a holy day has the unintended result of making no day holy, so the generalization of God results not in the general knowledge of God, but in no knowledge of Him whatsoever.

The scriptural record of God's revelation is a succession of stories, in each of which God makes Himself known by accommodation. Though it is true that God is everywhere, no story in Scripture portrays any patriarch, prophet, or apostle encountering God in such a manner. His revelation is always specific and particular. He can be named. The land of Israel is covered by places whose names are derived from specific encounters with God:

> Now Jacob went out from Beersheba and went
> toward Haran. So he came to a certain place and
> stayed there all night, because the sun had set. And
> he took one of the stones of that place and put it at
> his head, and he lay down in that place to sleep. Then
> he dreamed, and behold, a ladder *was* set up on the
> earth, and its top reached to heaven; and there the
> angels of God were ascending and descending on it.
>
> And behold, the LORD stood above it and said: "I *am*
> the LORD God of Abraham your father and the God of
> Isaac; the land on which you lie I will give to you and

your descendants. Also your descendants shall be as the dust of the earth; you shall spread abroad to the west and the east, to the north and the south; and in you and in your seed all the families of the earth shall be blessed. Behold, I *am* with you and will keep you wherever you go, and will bring you back to this land; for I will not leave you until I have done what I have spoken to you."

Then Jacob awoke from his sleep and said, "Surely the LORD is in this place, and I did not know *it*." And he was afraid and said, "How awesome *is* this place! This *is* none other than the house of God, and this *is* the gate of heaven!"

Then Jacob rose early in the morning, and took the stone that he had put at his head, set it up as a pillar, and poured oil on top of it. And he called the name of that place Bethel; but the name of that city had been Luz previously. Then Jacob made a vow, saying, "If God will be with me, and keep me in this way that I am going, and give me bread to eat and clothing to put on, so that I come back to my father's house in peace, then the LORD shall be my God. And this stone which I have set as a pillar shall be God's house, and of all that You give me I will surely give a tenth to You." (Gen. 28:10–22)

This familiar story of Jacob's encounter with God in a dream illustrates a number of the important points we have observed. First, Jacob's encounter with God in a dream is not amorphous. It is not the sound of a numinous voice or a generalized subjective impression. Jacob sees a ladder standing between heaven and earth. (Despite the ladder, Jacob's encounter is not an indication of a two-storey universe.

If you can go from this place to that by a ladder, you are still on the same metaphysical floor of the house.) Later Christians would make much of the meaning of this ladder. But for Jacob, that it is the Lord who appears at the top of the ladder and speaks to him is what matters most. We are not given a description of how God appeared to Jacob. Jacob alone probably knows that. But the words he hears are quite specific, as is his response: "Surely the LORD is in this place, and I did not know *it*."

Interestingly, Jacob has not confined God to a separate realm that has entered his head in some dreamlike state. For him, not only is the dream significant, but so is the place where he was sleeping when it occurred. His response is key: "And he was afraid and said, 'How awesome *is* this place! This *is* none other than the house of God, and this *is* the gate of heaven!'"

His response is thoroughly pre-modern. The dream and the encounter with God are not abstractions. God does not appear to him in general. The dream and the encounter are quite specific and particular, even encompassing the land on which he slept. Thus it is that Bethel, the "House of God," remains present in Israel to this day.

The experience of travel in the Holy Land, even in our modern times, retains this unique character. Holy places abound. For the Christian who is familiar with Scriptures and has any sense of devotion, walking through the Holy Land is just that—walking through the *Holy Land*. The presence of the secular (merchants, sellers of trinkets, barking bargainers) outside every holy place can seem disruptive and out of place. In this vein, I have been told that there is a plan by some American Christians to build a Bible theme park—not a place of holiness, but a place that one can visit that reminds one of a time long ago when Jesus walked the land and Israel was holy. Pure imagination—pure secularism. No God will be found there. He has been exiled from His own land into the second storey of man's imagination: the God of the theme park.

Such imaginary and second-storey devotions to God are foreign to the ethos of Christianity in its classical form—as in the case of Eastern Orthodox Christianity. Orthodox Christianity is, to a large extent, the Church of the shrines in the Holy Land. Everywhere one turns, there is another Orthodox Church, marking with devotion and prayer significant and particular places in the life and ministry of Christ. Nor are these places set aside as mere historical markers. They are places of prayer. Stories not unlike that of Jacob abound among the Christians who live in that doggedly one-storey land.

Many Orthodox Christians living in the modern world (and often other Christians as well) find the dominating secular aspect of culture to be at odds with their faith. Orthodox Christians are taught that the church building itself is holy—it is not just a place for members to assemble. It is, in New Testament terms, the temple whose plan was shown to Moses when he built the tabernacle in the wilderness. For these Christians, Moses' vision was but a shadow of the true tabernacle in heaven. The New Testament temple points yet more fully towards that heavenly pattern. Not only is the building considered holy, but within it there is the Holy Place—the space surrounding the altar—often demarcated by a screen of icons.

Just as in Jacob's dream and the other stories of divine encounters in Scripture, boundaries exist within the Church. Some places are accessible, and others are less accessible. Certain behaviors are appropriate for certain locations, whereas other behaviors are considered inappropriate and profane. This—the antithesis of secular space—exists so that one may encounter God as He has always been encountered: in specific and particular ways.

Of course, the most particular manifestation of God is His

incarnation as the God-man, Jesus Christ. Classical Christianity defends the particularity of that manifestation by insisting that icons (images) may be made of Him. The incarnate Christ is particular in such a way that we may paint His portrait. It is interesting that the Fathers of the Church declared that "icons do with color what Scripture does with words" (a statement we will explore in depth at a later point). It is a recognition that Scripture paints a very specific and particular portrait with its words.

Increasingly in our secularized world, the particularity of Scripture and of God Himself have come to offend the borderless imaginations of the secular world. Thus, God is made to carry new names that would exile Him further from the particularities of our world. A God whose name is Father/Mother is no one we would meet except in imaginary constructs of borderless minds. Such a designation pushes God further away. The second storey, which long ago became the playground of the imaginations of creative theologians, has become the habitation of God-as-you-imagine-him/her/it-to-be. Such a God, of course, is the God-who-is-not-there, because he is the God of our creation, rather than we of his.

If we are to know God in any manner that transcends our own imaginings, it will only be in the particularity of a one-storey world. In subsequent chapters, we will turn to many of the specific ways in which this God is so encountered.

CHAPTER FIVE

CHRISTIAN ATHEISM

This chapter's title seems to contain an inherent contradiction: How can one be both an atheist and a Christian? My purpose is to push our understanding of the problems inherent in a two-storey universe to the extreme. For to live in a world in which God is not everywhere present, or is present only in the most generalized fashion, is to live as a functional atheist.

Our system of belief has been reduced to little more than a set of ideas. The generalized God is useful only for argument and debate. Atheists, in certain bizarre cases, have proven that they are capable of inventing "religions" from their ideas and even winning converts. In history, one of the religious systems that often comes closest to what I describe as a two-storey universe is the philosophical account of the deists, who counted among their number many of America's founding fathers. These men, though often members of organized churches, still held to some form of deism: it was one of the dominant philosophies of the Enlightenment period during which the American nation was founded.

Their account of the universe was almost a pure two-storey world-view. In simple terms, God, or the "Deity" (as He was frequently named—thus avoiding sectarian debate over who God is), created the universe in its beginning, setting it in motion. The Deity did so in such a way that the universe performed according to immutable laws. These laws were God's "Providence." But the deists understood this providential creation very differently from any idea that God intervened in history in a providential way.

One of the more extreme examples of this philosophy is found in the thought and work of Thomas Jefferson. Jefferson produced a highly edited version of the Bible from which every reference to the miraculous had been expunged, every instance of the miraculous eradicated. What remained were the "pure" moral teachings of Christ, which for the deists was all that was of value in Scripture. That man ought to pray was not denied: creatures owed thanksgiving to their Creator.

The deists never succeeded in becoming a dominant or significant religious force, unless certain elements of the early Unitarian-Universalist movements are to be thought of as dominant in any way. But, as an expression of a major strain of thought in existence at the time, the deists had their influence through much of the culture.

Other than having some notion of an original Creator, deists were practical atheists. The God who created had completed His work. Ethics were as much a matter of scientific discovery as any other principle of physics. The deists believed in something they called "God" or "Providence," but only in a very divorced sense. It would be hard to distinguish their thought from that of an atheist, except that they clung to an idea of God, at least as the initiator of all things.

I have here introduced the notion of "practical atheism," meaning by it that, although a person may espouse a belief in God, it is quite possible for that belief to be so removed from everyday life that God's nonexistence would make little difference. This is certainly the most extreme form of God's exile to a second storey. God, reduced to idea or argument, is still no God at all, at least from the point of view of classical Christianity. God is not an idea.

Some forms of Christian fundamentalism fall within this description. I have had dialog with Christians for whom everything that can be known of God is to be found within Scripture itself. They have no direct knowledge of God—only the knowledge that can be derived and "proven" from Scripture. In some of these groups, reason is seen as the tool divinely given for obtaining such knowledge (this applies to a relatively small group within the larger Protestant picture). Such an approach is largely deist in structure, even if doctrine is allowed a place. However, doctrine has largely assumed an inferior place within an overall argument—the argument itself is the important thing.

If everyone agrees to hold their beliefs about God in a compartmentalized fashion—as a matter of belief understood as a set of ideas—then conflict is minimized.

Much more common is Christian atheism as a default position. This is the result of the secular culture standing in a dominant position. It is not an indication of liberalism or conservatism; it can exist in both worlds. Christian atheism is simply the hallmark of secularized Christianity. Remember that secularism was not born as an idea in itself, but as a reaction to the religious wars of various Christian groups in the sixteenth and seventeenth centuries. Secularism, in its infancy, was not designed as an enemy of Christian belief, but as a peaceful solution for Christians who had raised theological debate to the level of out-and-out warfare. It is an unintended effect that secularism has become a thing in itself, responsible for the exile of God from everyday life. The natural force of this understanding has been to devalue all external forms of religious devotion (where they can be seen and become matters of debate, or even warfare). If everyone agrees to hold their beliefs about God in a compartmentalized fashion—as a matter of belief understood as a set of ideas—then conflict is minimized.

The result of this inner discipline has been the continued devaluation of outward forms. Sacraments have become less definitive, both in meaning and application. Until somewhere in the latter half of the twentieth century, virtually all Christian churches practiced some form of closed communion. The sacrament of the Eucharist was open only to believers within that denomination and, many times, only to confirmed members of that denomination. In some cases, it was open only to members of that particular parish.

In the latter part of the twentieth century, the understanding of the Eucharist shifted (largely as a result of theological work done within the World Council of Churches Faith and Order Commission), resulting in a change from "closed communion" to "open communion." Thus, in most Protestant churches, all baptized Christians (or some other such generous invitation beyond the walls of the denomination) are welcomed to receive communion when they visit another Christian group. A few Protestant churches extend this invitation even to the unbaptized, while other Protestant groups have begun to debate such radical "hospitality" as a possibility. The Roman Catholic and Eastern Orthodox churches have not followed this "hospitality" model of communion and have retained their earlier positions.

The shift is more than a movement from sacrament as participation in the Body and Blood of Christ to sacrament as sign of hospitality. There is a significant movement from the sacrament existing as a definitive communion with God to the sacrament representing a necessarily vague encounter with the divine. The more particularly the sacrament is defined or understood, the less possibility it has to become a sign of hospitality. In the extreme form of hospitality, where even the unbaptized are welcome to receive, it is hard to see how the sacrament need have any connection with God. The atheist is welcome at the cup. It would quickly be answered that "this is indeed the very character of the love of God," but it is also the character of an empty cup. What is to be found in the universalized cup? Is there enough content to call it God?

Christianity that has purged the Church of the sacraments, and of the sacramental, has only ideas to substitute in their place. The result is the eradication of God from the world in all ways other than the theoretical. Even subtle idealizations of the sacraments can have the same effect. Of course, since much of modern Christianity functions on this ideological level rather than the level of communion with the God-who-is-among-us, much of Christianity functions in a mode of practical atheism. The more ideological the faith, the more likely its proponents are to espouse what amounts to a practical atheism.

The more ideological the faith, the more likely its proponents are to espouse what amounts to a practical atheism.

Even Orthodox Christianity, with its wealth of dogma and Tradition, could itself be translated into this model—I have encountered it (though rarely) in such a form. It is a falsification of the faith. Sacraments must not be quasi-magical moments in which a carefully defined grace is transmitted to us; they must, instead, have the capacity to unite heaven and earth. The medieval limitation of sacraments to the number seven comes far too close to removing sacraments from the world. Historically, Orthodoxy seems to have declared that there are seven sacraments solely as a response to Western Reform and Catholic arguments (indeed, there are Orthodox writings that describe sacraments in greater numbers). In some sense, everything is a sacrament—the whole world is a sacrament.

However, if we only say that the whole world is a sacrament, soon nothing will be a sacrament. Thus, the sacraments recognized as such by the Church should serve not just to point to themselves, but also to point to God and to everything around us. Holy Baptism must remain, but it should change all water as well. The Cross should change all trees, and so on. But baptism gives the definition: water does not define baptism. Neither do trees define the Cross. Nor does man define Christ. Christ defines what it is to be human.

The more truly sacramental becomes the Christian life, the more thoroughly grounded it is in the God-who-is-among-us. Such a God is indeed "everywhere present and filling all things." Our options are between such a God—as proclaimed in the New Testament—and a God who need be no God at all, for He is removed from us in every meaningful way.

At the Divine Liturgy, before approaching the communion cup, Orthodox Christians pray together:

> I believe, O Lord, and I confess that Thou art truly
> the Christ, the Son of the living God, who camest
> into the world to save sinners, of whom I am first. I
> believe also that this is truly Thine own most pure
> Body, and that this is truly Thine own precious
> Blood. Therefore, I pray Thee: have mercy upon me
> and forgive my transgressions, both voluntary and
> involuntary, of word and of deed, committed in
> knowledge or in ignorance. And make me worthy
> to partake without condemnation of Thy most pure
> Mysteries, for the remission of my sins, and unto life
> everlasting. Amen.

There is no hint of distance between us and God. At this point, having prepared for communion, having confessed our sins, we stand at the very center of the universe, before the God Who Is, before the

God with whom Moses conversed on Mt. Sinai, and we receive His true Body and Blood.

A very unconscious form of Christian atheism occurs in the daily management of parish life and ministry. Over time, business methods and management techniques have come to take their place within the life of the Church. There is, of course, nothing wrong with properly accounting for money and its use. But most of the assumptions of business management and methods are rooted in a highly secularized account of the world. Certain methods, properly applied, yield certain results. Such thinking applies to building buildings, but is also applied in many cases to managing people. In such models, a pastor himself soon becomes a manager—one with a specialty, but a manager nonetheless. The life of the Church is thus measured in "problems" and "conflicts," all of which require proper handling.

The problem with such assumptions is that they do not require God. An atheist managing his company is not discernible from a Christian pastor in such a setting. The pastor may pray, but not as an integral part of the life of the Church. A "successful" parish can thus be judged

A God who remains generalized and reduced to ideology is no God at all. Only the daily encounter with the living God, with all the messiness it entails, can rise to the name Christian.

by its well-managed conflicts and general tone of happiness. In its most crass examples, success is measured by income and attendance. None of this assumes that conflict may very well be a gift of God for our salvation, or that the day-to-day inner struggle of parishioners has anything to do with the Christian life. In my experience, salvation can often be quite messy and disruptive of certain aspects of parish life. Such "messiness," like God Himself, can easily be unwelcome in a "successful" parish of the secular model.

Like the sacraments, daily life becomes emptied of encounter with God. A God who remains generalized and reduced to ideology is no God at all. Only the daily encounter with the living God, with all the messiness it entails, can rise to the name *Christian*. The divine realism and immediacy of a one-storey universe makes bold claims about the nature of the God whom we worship and how we relate to Him. Its distance and remove from the "end-of-miracles" deism of some Biblicists could not be more complete.

There is a dialog that may take place between Christians and atheists. But there is, prior to that, an even more important dialog in which to be engaged, and that is with the practical atheism of Christians who have exiled God from the world around us. Such practical atheism is a severe distortion of the Christian faith and an extremely poor substitute for the real thing.

The late Richard John Neuhaus, Catholic priest and convert, wrote frequently of returning the Church to the public square. I think the problem is far deeper. In many cases we have to speak about returning God to the Church. Where practical atheism is the faith of a group of "believers," their presence in the public square makes no positive difference. What does it matter what believers whose God is as good as nonexistent think or say (as believers)?

Classical Christianity traditionally presents a God who cannot be exiled from our world, no matter how men try. He has come among us, and not at human invitation. "While we were yet sinners, Christ died for us" (Romans 5:8). He is already in the public square as the crucified God who is reconciling the world to Himself, whether we like it or not. The renunciation of practical atheism comes when we do the only thing the Christianity of a one-storey universe can do: keep the commandments of God and fall down and worship—for God is with us.

CHAPTER SIX

THE SHAPE OF A ONE- STOREY UNIVERSE

I opened this book with thoughts on the "shape" of the universe, and have suggested that the imagery of a two-storey universe is problematic for believing Christians. God is "everywhere present and filling all things." But if this is so, and the world is more properly thought of as single-storey, then the way we think of the world and the things in the world must certainly change. If the secular world has no place for the God of the Christians, then it will have no place for the Christians themselves. Christians must live in a way and learn a manner of understanding that allows the reintegration of the world. There are indeed other ways of seeing the world that are a very deep part of the Christian tradition. With this chapter we will begin examining some of those ways of seeing and understanding in greater detail.

The Orthodox priest and noted patristic scholar, Andrew Louth, writing in his book, *Discerning the Mystery* (Oxford Press, 1981, p. 98), says:

> If we look back to the Fathers, and the tradition, for inspiration as to the nature of theology, there is one thing we meet which must be paused over and discussed in some detail: and that is their use of allegory in interpreting the Scriptures. We can

see already that for them it was not a superfluous, stylistic habit, something we can fairly easily lop off from the trunk of Patristic theology. Rather it is bound up with their whole understanding of tradition as the tacit dimension of the Christian life: allegory is a way of entering the 'margin of silence' that surrounds the articulate message of the Scriptures, it is a way of glimpsing the living depths of tradition from the perspective of the letter of the Scriptures. Of course the question of allegory in the Fathers is complex (and often rendered unduly complicated by our own embarrassment about allegory): but whatever *language* the Fathers use to describe their exegetical practice (and there is no great consistency here), they all interpret Scripture in a way we would call allegorical, and *allegoria* is the usual word the Latin Fathers use from the fourth century onwards to characterize the deeper meaning they are seeking in the Scriptures.

I have quoted Louth at some length to make a point. His characterization of a search for a "deeper meaning" is a hallmark of classical Christian thought about the Scriptures. The Fathers do not always call this meaning "allegorical"; indeed, it was and is called by many names ("typological," "anagogical," "tropological," etc.). But the Fathers shared a sense that there was something behind or beyond the text that confronted them. This same attitude towards the biblical text can also be seen in the manner in which they perceived the entire world.

One of the dominant characteristics of the modern, secular world is its more or less literal view of reality. Things are just that: things. Things are what they are, and the only associations they may have with anything else are purely notional. If I personally associate two things, it does not mean that they actually have an association or relation; it simply means that I think of them in that manner. In the history of thought, this concept of the world is classically known as Nominalism (in formal philosophy Nominalism takes a number of forms). Interestingly, in the medieval period, those who held to the philosophy of Nominalism were said to be part of the *Via Moderna*, the first use of the word "modern." The world may be known according to the laws of physics, but in the modern understanding, there is nothing more to be known about the world than what can be known through physics. There is nothing within, between, or behind the world. There is just the world.

> *If there is nothing within, between, or behind the world, then we must place God and all that we call "spiritual" somewhere outside the world.*

It is this very literal character of the modern world that forces modern Christians into a two-storey worldview. If there is nothing within, between, or behind the world, then we must place God and all that we call "spiritual" somewhere outside the world.

This same modern way of viewing the world is often the way modern Christians view the Scriptures. Modern Christians tend towards literalism (whether from a fundamentalist or a liberal understanding). The meaning of a word, phrase, or passage in the text is ultimately to be found in the author's intention. Of course, there are a wide variety of ideas about how an author's intent may be found or whether such a thing is even possible. Fr. Louth refers to an approach to the Scriptures that sees every word, phrase, and passage as capable of more than its surface meaning. Indeed, in the writings of the Fathers of the Church, there always seems to be a movement to reach beyond the surface and into something yet deeper and richer.

Christ Himself has something like this in mind when, speaking to the religious leaders of His day, He says, "You search the Scriptures, for in them you think you have eternal life; and these are they which testify of Me" (John 5:39). It is among the most radical claims of Christ: He is the meaning of the Old Testament Scriptures. The classical Christian tradition followed this lead and looked for Christ within every passage of the Old Testament, including those that might seem least obvious.

This same possibility, inherent within the text of the Scriptures according to the classical Christian understanding, extends to the world itself. Thus the sacraments of the Church are not symbols in the modern sense of something that stands for something else—something that is not really there. Rather, they are symbols in the classical sense: two things that are brought together in a single reality. The very word *symbolos* in Greek means "to throw two things together." Interestingly, the opposite of *symbolos* in Greek is *diabolos*, which means "to divide."

The shape of the universe in this classical Christian understanding encompasses a world in which everything is capable of referring beyond itself and outside of itself.

The shape of the universe in this classical Christian understanding encompasses a world in which everything is capable of referring beyond itself and outside of itself. Everything becomes a doorway and a window, a means of participation in the depths of reality. I have often thought of this topic under the heading of *iconicity*—a word I use to connote the referential character, not just of the text we read, but of the world we inhabit. The world as pure object, as a collection of self-contained and self-explaining things (of which people are but examples), is foreign to the perception of traditional Christianity. Our culture may afford believers the luxury of believing that something has reference beyond itself, but it only does so as a courtesy, a social bargain. We allow others to infer meaning (where secularly none exists) simply out of respect for their will. If you want the world to be referential, the culture will respect that, remembering, however, that this is only "true for you."

The classical Christian claim is not the same thing as relativist courtesy. The text has a deeper meaning not because I infer it, but because I discern it. The meaning is real and true. Indeed, the classical Christian claim is that the truth of everything (not just of texts) is to be found precisely in its referential character and in that to which it refers.

To know the personal God is to know God in the manner in which persons are known. The content of a person always has an infinite quality, and this is especially so of God. And that content always has a referential quality as well. Thus, to know Christ is also to know Him as Son, and hence the Son of the Father. "No one comes to the Father but by Me," Christ says. For the person of the Father (as is indicated by the name revealed to us) is always referential to the Son (as the Son is to the Father).

And this must be said even of human persons. We never know each other exhaustively nor in the crass manner of modern objectivism. For each of us, fearfully and wonderfully made, is also infinitely referential. Thus knowledge of another is perhaps better described as *relation* or *participation*. It cannot mean *comprehension*.

The same is true of the text of Scripture. To read the text of Scripture without the constant and abiding sense that there is more here than I can see or understand is not to have read Scripture at all, or at least to have read it badly.

St. Antony the Great was once asked by a philosopher where his books were. He replied, "My book, O philosopher, is the world." St.

Paul also sees this aspect of creation: "For since the creation of the world [God's] invisible attributes are clearly seen, being understood by the things that are made, even His eternal power and Godhead" (Romans 1:20).

For much of the modern world, this capacity of creation has become the opacity of creation. We can see no further than the thing itself. Modern man is in danger of losing his ability to read the references of everything about him. And with that loss comes the diminution of everything, including himself.

The world and all that is in it is given to us as icon, not because it has no value in itself, but because the value it has in itself is the gift of God—and this is seen in its iconicity. Another person can be my entry into Paradise, or just as clearly my entry into Hades (and both in a far deeper sense than the merely moral). Love alone reveals things for what they are and transforms them into what they were always intended to be. Love alone reveals the true shape of the universe.

CHAPTER SEVEN

THE HALLWAY AT THE END OF THE WORLD

I recently had the opportunity to visit Holy Trinity Orthodox Church in Parma, Ohio, just outside of Cleveland, and to appreciate its iconography, which is a striking example of the modern renaissance that is taking place in construction and decoration of Orthodox churches across the world. Walls, ceiling—every visible surface of the church—is covered in iconography, making the building itself an architectural and iconographic proclamation of the Gospel of Christ. An unusual feature of the iconography at the parish is found in a hallway that connects the narthex of the church to the parish hall. The walls of the hallway are a single, continuous icon, in which the entire content of the Book of Revelation is depicted. To stand in the hallway is to stand in the midst of the fantastic images that fill that book: the Lamb on the Throne, the twenty-four elders, the beast with ten horns, the entire collection of the Apocalypse, along with selected passages of the text—all create an experience that is hard to describe. It is as if you were able to read the book in a matter of minutes. Of course, the icon will also reward careful views that would take hours.

This Orthodox experience reminded me of the atmosphere of my childhood. Southern evangelical Protestantism during the 1950s and '60s was dominated by themes of the end of the world. Headlines from the newspaper and events across the world were constantly conflated with the imagery of St. John's Revelation, the Book of Daniel, and other apocalyptic passages of the Bible. That the world stood dangerously close to a nuclear holocaust throughout that same period only heightened the perceived urgency of the preaching.

American culture has always been apocalyptic, though the apocalypse that informs our culture has not always been a story of impending disaster. America as the "Promised Land" was a far earlier story, utopian in nature and a powerful draw for some of the early English Puritan settlements. The same apocalyptic drive to a purer society, however, turned dark in the bloody Civil War of the 1640s in England, twenty years after Puritans had first come to North America.

The apocalyptic sense that accompanied the revolutions of the late eighteenth century (including both America and France) yielded to more religious versions by the 1830s and '40s. Apocalyptic religious groups began to flourish in various parts of the nation, from the Mormons to the Millerites, with the latter gathering repeatedly on mountaintops to await a predicted second coming of Christ.

Without giving the entire history of Darbyite interpretation of the Bible, which today forms the basis of Dispensationalism and which laid the original groundwork for popular expectations of the imminent return of Christ, it is possible to say that large portions of modern evangelical Protestantism would be unrecognizable without their strong mix of Bible prophecy and geopolitical commentary.

There is a common structure throughout the modern use of the apocalyptic: it is linear in shape. The landscape of the universe not only involves how we understand the objects and places around us, but also how we understand those things within the position of time. Our understanding of time has much to do with our understanding of the nature of truth. It also has very much to do with the character of the Christian faith.

In describing the modern Christian use of the apocalyptic as linear, I am describing it as essentially conceived as a series of events along a timeline of history, similar to other events along the same timeline. Those events that are seen as apocalyptic differ only in that they come at the end of that timeline. This is a radical departure from classical and Orthodox Christian understanding—a departure that seriously distorts the nature of the Christian faith.

History, conceived in a purely linear fashion, is similar to the literal conception of the secular universe. Events happen in succession, each one giving way to the next. What is in the past is inaccessible to us other than through historical research, theory, and guesswork. The future has not occurred and thus has nothing particularly to do with the present or the past. The nature

This historical captivity of the Christian mind has created only two options: fundamentalism and liberal revisionism.

of the linear view, particularly with its changeless view of historical events, tends to frame truth as something determined by events in the past. Thus, the question, "What is true?" generally means, "What actually happened?"

This historical captivity of the Christian mind has created only two options: fundamentalism and liberal revisionism. It is possible to posit a dogmatic character to history and to assert that everything in history occurs just as it is recorded in the Bible—and thus, the Bible is true. Or you can assert that history may be researched and interpreted independently of the Bible (generally yielding an interpretation that is determined by the present ruling cultural norms). In both cases, the Christian faith is held hostage to a view of history that forces either intellectual dishonesty or simplistic fideism, or else sacrifices every Christian norm and doctrine to the whims of whatever current research theories are popular. Neither option has a place within the classical Orthodox Christian understanding of time.

Four times in the Book of Revelation, Christ speaks and says, "I am the Alpha and the Omega." This declaration in its most complete form is found in 1:8: "'I am the Alpha and the Omega, *the* Beginning and *the* End,' says the Lord, 'who is and who was and who is to come, the Almighty.'"

In a certain fashion, the statement echoes the proclamation of the Holy Name given to Moses: "I am that I am." The "I AM" of the Old Testament is repeated numerous times in St. John's Gospel in a deliberate echo of the Divine Name. Icons of Christ in the Eastern Church identify Christ with the Greek words, *Ho On*, the second part of the phrase "I am that I am" in the Greek translation of the Hebrew text.

In the revelation of the holy name to Moses, the present tense is offered, and the full meaning of that tense is given in St. John's quotation, "[I am He] who is and who was and who is to come . . ." This is not a statement that God was, but is now past, that He is but will someday also be. Rather, this is the proclamation of the Lord of all time, who always is, always was, and always shall be.

Within the Christian proclamation of the Gospel, this relationship of God to time takes a particular shape. That shape is described as an eschatological relationship. *Eschaton* is the Greek word for the "end"— and *eschatology* means "the study of the last things." The classical, Orthodox understanding of the last things is not linear in character. It does not refer to those things which necessarily happen at the end of all the other things. Rather, Christ Himself is the eschaton (Rev. 1:17). He who is the end of all things is also the One who was before the beginning, and also the One who lived among us, was crucified in time, and is risen from the dead. Wherever He is—the End has come.

Within the teaching of the Fathers of the Church, this eschatology had a very specific application and structure. Both St. Ambrose in the

West and St. Maximus the Confessor in the East stated that truth is to be found in the Eschaton (the End—Christ Himself), while the New Testament is *image* or *icon*, and the Old Testament is *shadow*. This is a complete reversal of the linear, historical view of the modern secular world and the modern Christianity that has come to mirror it. The historical, linear model imprisons truth within the past as fact (*factus*— Latin for "what has been done"). Much of modern Christian thought has been shaped by the anxiety caused by the linear model—the truth is "trapped" in history within the modern understanding—creating a battle for the nature of historical understanding.

Classical Christian understanding has a proper eschatological shape. Just as the universe is a single storey, so time itself is not linear, but shaped, revealed, and given its meaning by its end, which has already made itself manifest within history. Thus the truth, who is Christ Himself according to the Christian witness, is not trapped within the confines of history. The Truth has encountered history and made Himself manifest in that moment, but the same Truth, as the End of all things, is free and able to make Himself manifest at every moment and at all time.

No aspect of the structure or shape of the world of believers could be more important than the element of time and how we are to see the things of God in this aspect. The reduction of time to a literal, linear model has been among the most reductionist occurrences in the course of Christian history and has distorted the nature of our relation with Christ perhaps more than any other occurrence, historic, ideological, or otherwise.

The memorialism of certain Reformation groups, in which the presence of Christ in the Eucharist is reduced to a simple remembrance on the part of believers, is among the most egregious examples of the triumph of linearity. Here, the Eucharist is celebrated, but the presence of Christ is reduced to historical memory, the weakest possible interpretation of His words and commandments and a deep distortion of the role of *anamnesis* (memory).

The nature of time does not easily fit into the metaphor of one-versus two-storey accounts of the universe. But if linearity is viewed in such an image, then it can be said to create a three-storey structure, only one storey of which is accessible to human beings—with the purpose, meaning, and essence of the Christian faith consigned elsewhere. We live in the present. If what is important, defining, and meaningful is the prisoner of the past, accessible only through ancient texts, then we live as orphans in time with only the written stories of our past as comfort. We have stories of a glorious future to come—all of which often pale for many in comparison to the sufferings of this present age.

> *The One who is to come is also the Lord who is present to us now, and the same Lord who was before the beginning and who was slain for our salvation.*

However, the Tradition speaks of Christ as the "truth that is to come." This is also the truth which has already come to us in His life, ministry, death, and resurrection, as well as the truth that continually abides with us in His Body, the Church.

Learning to live in a one-storey universe means also learning to live in a world in which we ourselves are not the prisoners of time. The One who is to come is also the Lord who is present to us now, and the same Lord who was before the beginning and who was slain for our salvation. In Him, the Church becomes a community that has a present time, but is also the community of the eschaton. This is the great witness of the Orthodox Church of the East. Its self-understanding is that it is "heaven on earth," the community of the faithful, gathered at the end of the age with the Lord who is to come. In its liturgy, it even speaks of the Second Coming in the past tense, not because it believes that event to have "already" happened, but because it understands that when it gathers together as Church, it stands at the end of all things.

This understanding of the presence of the End in the midst of the present (as well as the past) is the classical eschatology of the Christian Church. As the Fathers noted, truth is found at the end of all things:

> Beloved, now we are children of God; and it has not yet been revealed what we shall be, but we know that when He is revealed, we shall be like Him, for we shall see Him as He is. (1 John 3:2)

> Therefore judge nothing before the time, until the Lord comes, who will both bring to light the hidden things of darkness and reveal the counsels of the hearts. (1 Cor. 4:5)

This understanding does not negate the knowledge we have of the world in which we live. But it sets parameters on that knowledge and reveals its temporary and relative character. When we describe the world with the knowledge of science, we describe as best we can what we see and understand. This is not the same thing as saying we know the Truth of things. There is, even in the created order, an opaqueness that does not yield to us the full mystery of the things we see and know. In the words of St. Paul: "For now we see in a mirror, dimly, but then face to face. Now I know in part, but then I shall know just as I also am known" (1 Cor. 13:12).

There need be no conflict between what we know and what we shall know. Conflict only arises when we claim to know what we do not know. On the level of our daily lives, this understanding asks us not to look to the past for our meaning (though we can also discern the End within the past): we are not defined by our history but by our end. To know what we are, it is necessary to know what we shall be. Christ is, for us, both the icon of the Truth and the Truth of which He is the icon. To answer the question of what we shall be, the truth will only be found in Christ—who is both the revelation of God and also the revelation of what it is to be human. Fully God and fully man, He is our truth and the very definition of truth.

CHAPTER EIGHT

A ROOM WITH A VIEW

Dreams are interesting things. Our modern age either makes too little of them or too much, but mostly, we believe that our dreams are about us and the inside of our heads. Those who make too little of their dreams write them off to anxiety, wish-fulfillment, or other stresses of the day. Those who make too much of them remind me of Western believers in reincarnation, who always seem to have been somebody famous: these dreamers expect to find the meaning of the universe or something equally significant in the slightest symbol.

Dreams certainly have significance—and as shown in Scripture, they can indeed be sent by God. My favorite biblical dream is that of Jacob, who sees a ladder stretching into the heavens and angels going up and coming down. His reaction upon waking was to attribute the dream to the place in which he was sleeping: "This is none other than the gate of heaven and the house of God!" And, of course, good patriarch that he was, he erected a stone and anointed it with oil.

Years ago, some years before I became Orthodox, I had a dream in which I was in a church. Its construction was of log-timber and it seemed obvious to me (as things in dreams can seem obvious) that it was an Orthodox church. There were icons and lampadas (oil lamps), and a sizable crowd of people. What fascinated me about this dream-church were its many rooms. Everywhere you went there were steps up and steps down and rooms here and rooms there, and all of them full of people and icons and lampadas and the faint smell of incense and the low murmur of worship and prayers. I remember the dream lasting quite a while, but with nothing more significant than the many rooms—and how it felt to be there.

That feeling is what remained with me when I awoke and what remains with me to this day. The description I have given is probably the best I can do, for I have no words for how it felt, other than to say it felt like an Orthodox church—but an almost endless church. When I think of life in a one-storey universe, I am reminded of the church in my dream. There were no apparent ladders to heaven, but every room opened into another holy place, into another encounter with heaven on earth.

Few things play as large a role in the life of the Eastern Church as icons. These depictions of Christ and the saints—sometimes painted on wood, sometimes as murals on walls and ceilings or as beautiful mosaics—are invariably the first thing one sees when entering an Orthodox church. Icons are popularly referred to as "windows to heaven." This is one of the places where language breaks down. If you are using language in a two-storey world, "heaven" is the equivalent of "upstairs." It would thus be very peculiar to describe something as being a "window to upstairs." The very language of the Church shows that it means something quite different.

Icons are not windows to another world, per se, but a revelation of the truth of existence—an existence that is more than we may see at first encounter.

Icons are not windows to another world, per se, but a revelation of the truth of existence—an existence that is more than we may see at first encounter. When we paint an icon of a saint, the effort is to paint the saint in the truth of his or her life, not in his or her mere historical appearance. Thus the symbolism of the Byzantine style points us towards the holiness of a saint. The same thing could be achieved (perhaps) by writing the saint's life—but an icon does it with a single picture.

The same is true of icons depicting biblical scenes. The icon of the Crucifixion famously contains many elements that you would not literally have seen that day in Jerusalem; but if you knew the truth of all that was happening, then you would know all that is shown in the icon.

This is one of the great difficulties of our one-storey world. It's not that we live on the first floor and that's all there is—

The primary organ of vision for human beings is not the eye, but the heart. Our eyes will only see what our hearts will allow.

it's that we live on the first floor and we don't know the half of it. We do not realize the true nature of where we are or when we are. Icons frequently show us much about the world as it truly is. This is the character of much of the lives of the saints: they not only see what we see—they see much more. Indeed, we are told, "Blessed are the pure in heart, for they shall see God." This is not a notion that if you're pure in heart, someday you will die and see the Lord. Such a construction would completely misunderstand the verse.

The verse tells us that the primary organ of vision for human beings is not the eye, but the heart. Our eyes will only see what our hearts will allow. Thus we almost never see the truth of our enemies—as our language says, "We are blinded to the truth." Anger blinds. Hatred blinds. Greed blinds. Politics blind.

Thus a great part of the Christian vocation is living in such a way that we will be able to see more and more clearly the truth of our own existence and of the world around us. There are those (non-Orthodox) who view the making and venerating of icons as inessential in Christianity. They may be willing to tolerate such things but do not see them as necessary. Making and venerating icons, in the wisdom of the Church, is not only pleasant, but indeed necessary. The veneration of an icon is an essential part of actually seeing it. The persons or situations that are presented to us in an icon are situations that call for humility of heart and an attitude of reverence. In some cases, the reverence is so deep that we not only kiss the icon involved, we actually prostrate ourselves to the ground before we kiss it (this is the case with the Holy Cross and with the burial shroud of Christ).

We have a culture where people bow themselves before money, before food, before the flesh, before power, before almost anything but the things of God. Our hearts are thus poisoned, and our vision becomes clouded. We cannot see or judge anything correctly. We do not see or know the true God, nor do we see our neighbors for who they truly are. The only corrective is to live a life learning to rightly honor those things that should be honored. If kissing an icon seems foreign, it may be merely a cultural issue; but, mind you, ours is a culture that has not taught us how to honor the things of God.

When catechumens enter the Orthodox Church through baptism, they renounce the devil and have prayers of exorcism read over them. Then they turn towards the East, towards the altar of God, and are told to worship Him. At that point they bow to the ground for the first time. They are then given the Creed to recite. There is an understanding that unless you bow down to the Lord God and worship Him, the words of the Creed will remain closed to you. You will not hear them rightly nor find them to be for your salvation.

Icons reveal something about the character of the world in which we live. They reveal that there is a distortion within us such that what things seem to be is not what they are. Icons are windows to heaven but also windows to the Truth, and thus, also, windows into the truth of our selves. The fact that icons cannot be truly seen without also being venerated points to the fact that our perception of the world and reality is also rooted in our relationship with the world and reality. Perceiving the truth is not an abstract, gnostic exercise, but a function of love and of holding things in their proper place of honor.

The veneration of icons not only reveals the truth of our existence—the hatred of icons reveals a great darkness within us and within the history of human culture. At various times and places, often with political or religious justification, outbreaks of iconoclasm (the "smashing of icons") have marred the peace of the world. One of the first such outbreaks occurred in the Byzantine Empire during the seventh and eighth centuries—at a time coterminous with the rise of Islam, which is also iconoclastic. There is a debate among historians as to whether the two movements had a direct connection. This early form of Byzantine iconoclasm gave rise to the Church's formal defense and definition of the theology of icons. Iconoclasm is a strange manifestation of human sin that has as its driving force—and hence, its allurement—the claim that it is defending the honor of God.

> *Perceiving the truth is not an abstract, gnostic exercise, but a function of love and of holding things in their proper place of honor.*

The icon smashers are as varied as certain forms of Islam or certain forms of Puritanism (and some of its Protestant successors). Some icon smashers direct their attention to pictures or statues *per se*, while others turn their attention even to ideological icons, such as the honoring of certain days and holidays.

It seems striking to me that iconoclasm has almost always accompanied revolutions. I suppose those who are destroying the old and replacing it with the new have a certain drive to "cleanse" things. During China's Cultural Revolution, books, pictures, older faculty members—indeed, a deeply terrifying array of unpredictable things and people—became the objects of the movement's iconoclasm. As in all revolutions, iconoclasm kills.

During the Protestant Reformation, iconoclasm was a frequent accompaniment of theological reform. Statues, relics, furniture—all became objects of destruction (as well as people). Some of this was state-sponsored, as was the original iconoclastic period. The logic of iconoclasm, however, cannot always be confined. In the Reformation, the logic of reform moved from destruction of images to destruction of the state (which was itself an icon of sorts). In Germany the result was the Peasants' Revolt, which became so dangerous to the powers that be that even Martin Luther had to denounce it and bless the state's bloody intervention.

In England the Reform that was first put in place by the state remained unsteady for over a hundred years. Eventually, the Puritan Reform (which took the logic of Reform to its next step) began to smash images, behead kings, depose bishops, forbid holidays, and even outlaw dancing. For ten years England was ruled by a bloody religious dictatorship that was as ruthless in its iconoclasm as any regime in history.

One particular scripture verse that appeals to many iconoclasts seems to condone their zeal:

> For though we walk in the flesh, we do not war according to the flesh. For the weapons of our warfare *are* not carnal but mighty in God for pulling down strongholds, casting down arguments and every high thing that exalts itself against the knowledge of God, bringing every thought into captivity to the obedience of Christ, and being ready to punish all disobedience when your obedience is fulfilled. (2 Cor. 10:3–6)

Of course, the verse is referring to sinful thoughts and uses martial imagery (as is not unusual in St. Paul). That same imagery applied to the governing of a state (or a church) can be quite dangerous. It is useful in the spiritual life, provided it is well directed by a mature and generous guide.

The plain truth of the matter is that God is an icon-maker. He first made man "in His own image." And in becoming man, the man He became is described as the "image of the invisible God" (Col. 1:15). The same God who gave the commandment to make no graven images also commanded the making of the cherubim on the Ark of the Covenant, as well as the images of angels woven in the curtain of the Tabernacle. He commanded the making of the image of the serpent lifted on a staff which brought healing to all who looked on it (an Old Testament prefiguration of the crucified Christ).

> *The plain truth of the matter is that God is an icon-maker.*

The Tradition of the Church knows the restraint that is inherently involved in offering honor. Orthodox Christian living requires that we know how to worship God with what is due to Him, but at the same time to know how to honor those things that are honorable without giving them what belongs to God alone. It is easy to say "give honor to God alone," but this is contrary to the Scriptures, in which we are told to "give honor to whom honor is due" (Romans 13:7; see also 12:10). We cannot honor God by destroying the very images He has created (and here I include the saints, who could not be what they are but by God's grace).

There is within iconoclasm a spirit of hatred and anger. Without them destruction would not be so easy. But such spirits are not of God—though they are easily attributed to zeal or excused as exuberance. Iconoclasm is not the narrow way, but the wide path of destruction. It is easy to declare that all days are the same and that no days should be considered holier than others. It is easy to check out the historical pedigree of every feast of the Church and declare that some had pagan predecessors. Of course some had pagan predecessors—as did every last human being. If the Church has blessed a day and made it to be a day on which an action of Christ, an event in His life, or a saint of the Church is to be honored and remembered, then it is acting well within the divine authority given it in Scripture (Matt. 18:18).

The only image that needs to be discarded is the one we have of ourselves as God.

More importantly, we will grow more surely into the image of Christ by imitating His actions and learning to build up rather than to smash. Giving place to anger and the spirit of iconoclasm, in all its various guises, has never produced saints, but only destruction that eventually has to give way to something more sane. The legacy of our culture's image-smashing (a powerful part of the Puritan world) is secularization—though now replete with its own images. If we fail to give a proper account of the role that images play in Christianity, the result will not be a Christianity with no images, but simply the dominance of cultural images and a subtle conformity to the world. The only image that needs to be discarded is the one we have of ourselves as God. We are not He. Worship God. Give honor to whom honor is due.

It is easy for reform movements to smash and destroy. Creating art and revealing the beauty and truth of the world in which we live is a difficult thing, requiring the best and deepest of man's devotion to God. God has given us windows to heaven and an opportunity to become the kind of people who can themselves become images of that heavenly reality. As we do so, the earth becomes ever larger and humanity ever more full. We find God among us.

CHAPTER NINE

THE LITERAL TRUTH

"Icons do with color what Scripture does with words." This is part of the formal declaration of the Seventh Ecumenical Council, a council that defended the making and veneration of icons in the Church. There was an easy consensus among the Christians of the day about what Scripture does with words. The Council was meeting to settle the question of what icons do with color. Today, we are in a very different setting: we have no consensus about what Scripture does with words, and most Christians have no idea about icons and their colors. But the simple statement of the Seventh Council gives something of a roadmap for understanding how the Scriptures can and should be approached—just as we have seen that icons themselves point towards a way of seeing the world.

I have, on occasion, stretched the word "literal" to describe certain aspects of the modern world and its self-understanding. It is, of course, a term that primarily belongs to the realm of reading. How do we read and understand a text? But in our modern world there is a very strong correlation between how we "read" the world and our place in it and how we tend to read texts. When literalism is applied to a text, it presumes that the text is all there is, and that its meaning is to be found, at most, within the intent of its author. Thus texts, particularly those that have something of a historical character, are seen much as we see a newspaper: they are to be judged according to their faithfulness to the "facts."

I have noted that the modern world has a distinctly historical cast. The period in which we live is seen both as a product of and as a reaction to all that has come before it. Just as we tend to see the world as a series of causes and effects, so we see history as describable as a series of causes and effects.

The literal character of these things is found in their self-referential nature. A word means what it means. A story is a story. The significance of a word or a story is to be found within the context of historical cause and effect. This literal character reduces stories to the level of "facticity" and values everything by its place within the chain of cause and effect. Time has a literal character as it extends itself—one thing leading to the next until all causes and effects have been exhausted.

The literal-historical reading of Scripture fulfills one of the fantasies of the modern world: we are in charge of everything around us—the masters of our world. Understanding history and its chain of cause and effect gives the illusion that we are able to understand the present causes within our world (and especially those things that we ourselves might cause) and thus to predict the effects (and achieve our own desired effects). In many ways it is the essence of secularism. Secularism can grant the existence of God (on a theoretical level) and make room for people to hold such an existence within their set of beliefs, but the world must be understood to work in a fashion that may be comprehended without reference to God. Cause and effect—and our ability to know, understand, and manage cause and effect—are critical. This alone, within the secular view, leaves man free.

On the other end of the scale, Christian fundamentalism is also committed to the same historical view and assessment of texts. However, its doctrinal commitments require that the texts be infallible in their historical content and utterly reliable. History, science, and all things that have an independent ascendency within modern liberal culture have a secondary and derivative position within Christian fundamentalist modern culture. If the text says that Joshua prayed and the sun stopped, then it must be historically and physically true that Joshua prayed and the sun stopped. If the text says Jonah was swallowed and spat up by a large fish, then historically it must be the case that Jonah was so swallowed and spat up. That the sun stopped and that Jonah was swallowed by a fish are themselves less important than the certainty that they happened. The meaning of the text has been lost in its "facticity." What is important about the text is that it is reliable. Its meaning has been collapsed by the historical argument and the secular model of the nature of truth.

It is this aspect of the literal character of truth that I have likened to a two-storey universe.

It is this aspect of the literal character of truth that I have likened to a two-storey universe. The lower-storey world we inhabit is of a singular, uniform character—the same for believer and unbeliever, not only in perception but in reality. Believer and unbeliever meet on a level playing field. Their conversation is within the same world, and its character is not in question. Whether God exists and intervenes in the playing field of the world is a matter of debate—but it is a debate removed from the world itself. Once the unbeliever announces his rejection of a second storey, conversation about belief in God has largely come to an end—other than to debate the existence of a second storey.

"Icons do with color what Scripture does with words": Those who wrote and interpreted the Scriptures were the same ones who painted and understood the icons. The icons are among many things that point us to a way of seeing the world and reading the Scriptures that integrates the spiritual life into a one-storey universe and makes it possible for us to understand our world in a manner that is in harmony with that of classical Christianity.

The traditional Byzantine form of iconography makes use of inverse perspective, a technique that makes the icon "open out" as we look deeper into it, rather than disappearing at some point of perspective in the background. For the modern eye, this can make the picture appear flat or somehow disproportionate. It is a technique developed by highly skilled artists who were no strangers to the realistic perspective of painting with which we are more familiar. Their technique was an effort to develop an artistic grammar that would have expression in line and color and that would speak in the same manner as Scripture does in word and letter. The resulting iconographic technique gives insight into the character of icons as well as the character of Scripture. The Seventh Council was able to declare that "icons do with color what Scripture does with words" precisely because both speak in an "iconic" manner—or we could say that icons speak in a "Scriptural manner." They are revelatory of one another—however, literalism is descriptive of neither.

The iconic character of Scripture begins to be apparent when one pays attention to how the New Testament "reads" the Old. Whenever Christ quoted or cited Scripture, He was referring to the writings that Christians now call the Old Testament. They were the Scriptures as far as the disciples were concerned. But the stories of the Gospel make it quite clear that the disciples did not understand how Christ Himself was related to the Old Testament, even though He said, "These [Scriptures] are they which testify of Me" (John 5:39). Instead, we have stories in the Gospels of the disciples' encounters with Christ after the resurrection, in which "beginning with Moses and all the prophets, He expounded to them in all the Scriptures the things concerning

Himself" (Luke 24:27). A literal reading of the Old Testament would not have required such exposition—nor remained utterly opaque after three years of discipleship.

Instead, there is an iconic quality to the Old Testament (and to the New) which renders its meaning obscure until the structure and meaning of the central icon of the Gospel is itself made clear. That icon is the Pascha of Christ. Today, "Pascha" is used in the same way as the English word "Easter." But its original meaning is much larger. The Pascha of Christ is the Passover of Christ. The Passover of the Jews is a story that must begin with their slavery in Egypt, the calling of Moses, his confrontation with Pharaoh, the plagues, culminating in the night of Passover itself, when Israel is "passed over" by the angel of death, and the night when Israel "passes over" the Red Sea on dry land and Pharaoh and his army are destroyed. All of this is Israel's Passover.

> *There is an iconic quality to the Old Testament . . . which renders its meaning obscure until the structure and meaning of the central icon of the Gospel is itself made clear. That icon is the Pascha of Christ.*

Christ's Passover, His Pascha, includes the entire economy of our salvation: His incarnation and birth from the Virgin Mary, His baptism and ministry, His betrayal and arrest, His mocking, scourging, and crucifixion, and His burial and resurrection on the third day, and, in subsequent understanding, His destruction of sin and death by His death and resurrection.

The Paschal shape of the Gospel was not understood nor accepted by heretical groups, such as the early gnostics. It was, however, a hallmark of the early Apostolic Church. St. Irenaeus, writing in the late second century, offers this observation about Paschal reading which shaped what he called the apostolic hypothesis:

> If anyone reads the Scriptures [that is, the "Old
> Testament"] in this way, he will find in them the Word
> concerning Christ, and a foreshadowing of the new
> calling. For Christ is the 'treasure which was hidden in
> the field' (Mt 13:44), that is, in this world—for 'the field
> is the world' (Mt 13:38)—[a treasure] hidden in the
> Scriptures, for He was indicated by means of types and
> parables, which could not be understood by men prior
> to the consummation of those things which had been
> predicted, that is, the advent of Christ. . . . And for this
> reason, when at the present time the Law is read to
> the Jews, it is like a fable; for they do not possess the
> explanation [*tên exêgêsin*] of all things which pertain
> to the human advent of the Son of God, but when it
> is read by Christians, it is a treasure, hid in a field, but
> brought to light by the Cross of Christ. (*Against the
> Heresies*, 4.26.1)

The Pascha of Christ is to be found in the Old Testament by means of "types" and "parables" which "could not be understood by men prior to the consummation of those things which had been predicted." The Pascha of Christ, and its unique understanding given to the Apostolic Church, was the primary "icon," the "type" and "parable" by which the Old Testament Scriptures were to be understood.

This not only provides the key for understanding the Scriptures but also provides a model for how the Scriptures are to be seen. Read literally, they will not yield the Pascha of Christ. Instead, they are a "treasure hidden in a field." From its inception, Christianity has offered both a unique reading of the Scriptures and a unique reading of the world. The literal quality of the modern world is foreign to the Gospel of Christ. When it is applied to the Gospel, the result is distortion and misunderstanding—not only of the Gospel itself, but also of the character of the world in which we live.

Two of my favorite examples of this Paschal-shaped understanding of the world and the Scriptures are found in the story of Jonah and the Whale and in the Gospel accounts of the Baptism of Jesus. Christ spoke repeatedly of His resurrection on the third day. Most Christian readers assume that this was a clear reference to some form of literal prophecy in the Old Testament. And yet, such a prediction is nowhere to be found. Instead, the single reference to His three-day resurrection is to be found in the figure (or "type") of the story of Jonah and the Whale. Christ Himself makes the connection: "For as Jonah was three days and three nights in the belly of the great fish, so will the Son of Man be three days and three nights in the heart of the earth" (Matthew 12:40).

Of course, He does not explain at the time what He means by the "Son of Man" being three days and nights in the heart of the earth. The words of Jonah could easily have been spoken by Christ in the "belly" of the earth:

> "For You cast me into the deep,
> Into the heart of the seas,
> And the floods surrounded me;
> All Your billows and Your waves passed over me.
> Then I said, 'I have been cast out of Your sight;
> Yet I will look again toward Your holy temple.'
> The waters surrounded me, *even* to my soul;
> The deep closed around me;
> Weeds were wrapped around my head.
> I went down to the moorings of the mountains;

The earth with its bars *closed* behind me forever;

Yet You have brought up my life from the pit,

O LORD, my God." (Jonah 2:3–6)

None of this seems clear until Christ's Pascha has occurred and His disciples have been instructed in its shape, form, and meaning. Indeed, we do well to remember that the Gospels are written after Pascha and are themselves utterly shaped by that event.

Such an observation can be deeply disturbing for historical literalists, for their faith rests within history and relies on the Bible as a literal recounting of history. The suggestion that the event of Pascha itself may have shaped the telling of the Gospel in any way creates waves of doubt, for it is not Pascha that shapes their belief, but a theory about the nature of history.

The story of Christ's Baptism is a very rich source for classical Christian reflection. Icons of this event carry layers of reference and meaning, portraying within one single icon whole chapters of biblical material and a wealth of theological understanding. In the fullest portrayal of the icon, Christ stands in the midst of the Jordan, with two board-like objects beneath His feet and snakes appearing around the edges of the boards. St. John the Baptist stands on one shore, angels on the other. A tree with an axe embedded in it appears in one corner. The entire scene is set at a stylized river, with towering walls framing the scene, often with a background of black.

It is a very striking icon, and unintelligible apart from the Pascha of Christ. In the Paschal reading of the icon, the Jordan River is the very edge of Hades, death, and hell. The towering walls framing the icon, often accompanied by a background of black, artistically echo the icon of Christ's Descent into Hades. Thus His Baptism is a foreshadowing of that descent and His defeat of sin and death. The serpents who appear at the edges of the board-like objects are the demons of hell; the boards, the very gates of Hades themselves, an image that appears again in the icon of Christ's Descent into Hades. The serpents echo Psalm 74:13, in which God "crushes the heads of the dragons in the waters." Thus the Baptism of Christ iconically foreshadows the whole of His Pascha. By the same token, the whole of our salvation is summed up in this biblical image:

> Or do you not know that as many of us as were baptized into Christ Jesus were baptized into His death? Therefore we were buried with Him through baptism into death, that just as Christ was raised from the dead by the glory of the Father, even so we also should walk in newness of life. For if we have been united together in the likeness of His death, certainly we also shall be *in the likeness* of *His* resurrection, knowing this, that our old man was crucified with *Him,* that the body of sin might be done away with, that we should no longer be slaves of sin. For he who has died has been freed from sin. Now if we died with Christ, we believe that we shall also live with Him, knowing that Christ, having been raised from the dead, dies no more. Death no longer has dominion over Him. For *the death* that He died, He died to sin once for all; but *the life* that He lives, He lives to God. Likewise you also, reckon yourselves to be dead indeed to sin, but alive to God in Christ Jesus our Lord. (Romans 6:3–11)

Within the meager narrative of the Baptism of Christ in the Gospels, on a literal level, the event can be understood as little more than the inauguration of Christ's ministry. But the icons of the event (Theophany) point to a far deeper understanding—an understanding that is reflected in Romans 6. Our baptism is a union with Christ's crucifixion and resurrection. In the iconic treatment of Christ's baptism, the event itself is a foreshadowing and a participation in that very death and resurrection. Such a reading would be lost in a merely literal treatment of the account. But the early Church's understanding, reflected in the icon of the event, points to deeper levels of meaning. To a degree, Christ's baptism in the Jordan *is* Christ's Pascha, at least in a proleptic or foreshadowed sense.

It is little wonder that the disciples did not understand until they had been taught. But the Gospels as we have them are the writings of the apostles after they had been taught. They are a thoroughly Pascha-shaped telling of the story, even as Christ's death and resurrection revealed to them a Pascha-shaped universe. Pascha is decisive and revelatory of all that is, so that St. John can refer to Christ as the "lamb slain from the foundation of the world" (Rev. 13:8). The foundation of the world itself is built upon the Pascha of Christ.

Reading the Scriptures is a lesson in "reading" the world, for Christ's Pascha did not occur as a mere literary event, but happened within our world and its space and time. Just as that event revealed the Scriptures to have their proper meaning given by the shape of Pascha itself, so, too, our world has been revealed to have been founded upon Pascha. We cannot remove Christ's resurrection to a place of meta-meaning, a second storey where religious truth dwells. It is the foundation of everything we see and experience and reveals the world to be what it is.

Thus, neither we nor the world should be thought of as literal, if by that one means what the modern world thinks of the term. St. Nikolai Velimirovich is quoted as saying, "A man is not that which can be put into a grave, but is rather that which the universe cannot contain." I would add to that—that the universe itself is not the sort of thing that can be "contained"; it has layers upon layers of meaning and possibilities that are only revealed in the presence of Christ. We are meant for more than we can literally imagine.

CHAPTER TEN

THE MYSTERY OF PERSONS

I remember being startled the first time I read the saying of St. Silouan the Athonite (twentieth century): "The criterion for the presence of the Holy Spirit, the criterion of the truth, is the love for one's enemies."[2] I have elsewhere seen the thought (or simplified it in my own mind) in this form: "You only know God to the extent that you love your enemies." I believe it is true, and also that it is perhaps the most significant thing we can understand in the journey of our Christian life. There are many things to occupy our thoughts and our energies—the Christian life offers endless space for exploration. But if, in the end, it has not resulted in knowing God, then it has been a useless exercise and a life that missed its purpose. And if you can only know God to the extent that you love your enemies—then there can probably be nothing of greater importance.

Of course, such a thing is not easy. However, in its difficulty we see the depths of the problem that confronts our life with God. We have a difficult time loving those who love us, let alone those who hate us.

The statement of St. Silouan was realized quite deeply in his own life, according to his biographer, the Elder Sophrony Sakharov of St. John's Monastery in Essex, England. St. Silouan entered into depths

---

2   Quoted by Archimandrite Zacharias in *The Enlargement of the Heart*, Mt. Tabor Publishing, 2006.

of prayer for the world, including the enemies of God, on a level that can only be compared to that of the greatest of saints. Somehow, the life of all, great sinners included, became his life, because Christ had made them His own.

Perhaps the most devastating effect of the modern world for its inhabitants is its tendency to erode the fullness of what it means to be a person created in God's image. Just as we see the things about us to be no more than objects, we tend to see one another as little more than objects—objects that can think and choose. We do not see the true character of our lives—whether those of others or our own.

> *Perhaps the most devastating effect of the modern world for its inhabitants is its tendency to erode the fullness of what it means to be a person created in God's image.*

The truth of a person is always more than the person himself knows and always more than anyone else knows. Created in the image of God, human beings have an inherent transcendence. The soul is a mystery.

In Scripture we have hints of this mystery:

> For what man knows the things of a man except the spirit of the man which is in him? Even so no one knows the things of God except the Spirit of God. (1 Cor. 2:11)

> Set your mind on things above, not on things on the earth. For you died, and your life is hidden with Christ in God. When Christ *who is* our life appears, then you also will appear with Him in glory. (Col. 3:2–4)

> Beloved, now we are children of God; and it has not yet been revealed what we shall be, but we know that

when He is revealed, we shall be like Him, for we
shall see Him as He is. (1 John 3:2)

And perhaps my favorite such passage:

Where can I go from Your Spirit?
Or where can I flee from Your presence?
If I ascend into heaven, You *are* there;
If I make my bed in hell, behold, You *are there.*
If I take the wings of the morning,
And dwell in the uttermost parts of the sea,
Even there Your hand shall lead me,
And Your right hand shall hold me.
If I say, "Surely the darkness shall fall on me,"
Even the night shall be light about me;
Indeed, the darkness shall not hide from You,
But the night shines as the day;
The darkness and the light *are* both alike *to You.*
For You formed my inward parts;
You covered me in my mother's womb.
I will praise You, for I am fearfully *and* wonderfully
        made;
Marvelous are Your works,
And *that* my soul knows very well. (Psalm 139:7–14)

We are "fearfully and wonderfully made." This simple statement also
implies that each person should be approached in "fear and wonder"
(in the biblical sense of "fear") if we are to have any chance of properly
seeing and knowing him. It is all too easy to diminish one another
to little more than one-storey beings—objects of desire or objects

to consume our products. When others are seen in such a way, only power matters. Every human being can be seen as a challenge and a threat, a competitor. Friends become very few, and enemies multiply relentlessly. Civil discourse becomes impossible.

But this is not the truth of our being. Fearfully and wonderfully, we are made in the image of God, even though this largely remains a mystery. The commandments of the Gospel—love, patience, kindness, forgiveness of all for everything—are more than a moral road map of good behavior. They are a description for living the truth of our existence.

It is this transcendent truth of our existence that is depicted in the holy icons of the Eastern Church. The "grammatical" rules for painting ultimately work to create an artistic/theological model for Christ, the saints, plants, and animals that reveals and makes present this transcendent reality. As noted earlier, a large part of that artistic grammar is the use of inverse perspective. The painting opens ever outward as you look at it, rather than disappearing in a distant point of perspective. In the same way, the truth of our being does not disappear in some point of finitude, but opens ever outward as we extend ourselves towards God and others in the communion of love.

I remember a song written by a friend—a college classmate—that began with the line, "My life wouldn't make a movie." His lament was that he seemed to himself to be less than interesting. I would counter that movies are too small. The wonder of him could not fit on the screen.

The fearful wonder that is our salvation in Christ is rooted both in God's goodness and in what it means to exist as person. Our modern world is sometimes castigated for having made human beings the center of everything. This is only true if we measure our modern world by its economics and its entertainment industry. In truth, the modern world has often reduced what it is to be human. At one extreme there are those who reduce the beginning of human life—truly fearful and wonderful—to euphemisms of biological insignificance. Others reduce the restrictions of old age and ill-health to conditions that make life "not worth living." In the interim, people are often reduced to decision-makers ("shoppers" in its lowest form). In some Christian accounts, the actions of the human will are utterly paramount. We "choose" Christ. Doubtless, our choices are important. But the human will is fear-fully and wonderfully made and cannot be easily described, even if it is all too easily manipulated.

> *To exist as a person . . . is to exist by love. Thus, there must be others to love.*

We exist as persons solely by love. In theology, it is understood that it is love that creates the distinction between human beings as mere individuals and human beings as truly personal, created in the image of God. An individual need love no one and no thing. An individual exists like a rock (forgive me, Paul Simon). It is not the proper mode of existence for a human being created in God's image—but it is a mode of existence that sin has birthed in us. Love is a struggle.

To exist as a person, however, is to exist by love. Thus, there must be others to love. For this reason it is said that one cannot exist as a person by himself alone. It is also the reason that ultimately we must love our enemies and all who exist—for not to love someone is to deny our own true existence. When sin entered the world, among its first results was murder, and necessarily so. In a manner of speaking, Cain did not kill his brother—he couldn't even see Abel as his brother. Before God he renounced any responsibility for his brother. Since love is a gift from God and not something we create ourselves (at least the love by which we truly exist as persons), it is without limit. Every act of love extends the very fabric of our being.

EVERYWHERE PRESENT

I can recall in the early years of my marriage having conversations with my wife as our family grew. Having the first two children was a relatively easy decision. However, there were and are many subtle cultural pressures to stop at two. Nevertheless, we had four (thank God!). One of the absurd thoughts that crossed my mind during that time was, "Will I be able to love more children if we have them?" The thought is rooted in a concept of love as a limited commodity and the heart as unable to grow. Quite the opposite is true. The more we love, the greater our capacity for yet more love. It is possible to love, even on the personal level, the entire universe—and not as a mere abstraction. When you read the life of St. Silouan, you realize that his love for all is also a love for each. He exists in something approaching the fullness of personhood. My enemy is not only someone I am commanded to forgive and to love—he is also the means of my existence. The commandment to love your enemies is a voice in the darkness crying, "Let there be light."

CHAPTER ELEVEN

A LIFE OF CAREFUL DEVOTION

The religious life of the modern world, divided into two stories, is a world of make-believe. The false reality posited by the secular worldview, when unchallenged by the Christian life, presents an atmosphere that is toxic to the life of believers. We too easily believe that "reality" means the "hard stuff" around us, but generally does not include our religious beliefs. We live in the neutral zone—the first floor of the universe, where only a suspension of the natural law will yield contact with God.

This bifurcation of the universe is by no means an inheritance of the Christian tradition. Instead, it is the legacy of the late years of Western civilization, a by-product of the Reformation and the popular response to its ideas. It is, or will be, the death of much of the Christian world unless it is resisted and renounced. In time, those who live in this manner will either cease to believe in God or will find that their children have abandoned Him—or left the faith to find Him elsewhere, having concluded that Christianity is bankrupt.

The intention I have had in writing about these various aspects of the Christian Tradition and their importance is the resurrection in hearts and minds of the belief in a one-storey universe. Our hearts need to come to the fixed conclusion that *God is everywhere present*— that He is more real than the things we may think of as "real" and is deeply and utterly committed to our transformation into the image of His beloved Son.

Any Christianity that embraces a less-integrated worldview is rendered increasingly powerless. It is a Christianity whose God exists only in an abstract sense. Such a life is madness in the end. It cannot but be encumbered with doubt while fostering opinion and argument in the place of faith. The result is an intellectualized faith (however simple or sophisticated), always driven by the culture, either in ignorant subservience or in whatever form its political masters direct for the "culture wars." What Christianity in its various secularized forms has not done and cannot do is to produce true culture. The production of culture is not the goal of the Christian faith, but a faith that is truly integrated and grounded in the God who is everywhere present cannot help but produce culture—for it produces a whole humanity.

The classical tradition of the Church, throughout its history, has believed and taught that fasting, prayer, repentance and tears, obedience, and radical forgiveness of everyone for everything are tools given us by God for our cooperation with His work of grace, and that such spiritual labors yield fruit—"some a hundredfold, some sixty, some thirty" (Matt. 13:8). Those who have lived in the fullness of that tradition have hungered for the Kingdom of God and believed with all their heart that it was possible to enter that blessed state to some degree in this lifetime.

True Christianity is not a faith in abstractions, nor is it about a reward, up there, someday. It is as real as the Incarnation of the Word. It is as real as the leper healed by Christ. It is as real as the storm He calmed from the boat. It is as real as the nails that held His flesh on the cross. No abstractions. Christ's resurrection is not the victory of abstraction over reality, but the victory of Reality over the delusion of death and all its kingdom. It is the union of earth and heaven, created and uncreated. In such a union, there cannot be two metaphysical floors of reality.

It will sound somewhat silly for me to suggest that we learn to pray to God as if He really exists. Of course, God really exists. But the habits of the heart within a two-storey universe harbor deep and secret doubts about that very existence. True asceticism and devotion hungers for the Kingdom of God above all else, present among us, knowing that it is the only proper ground of our being.

God has become man, and in that event the abstraction of our schismatic existence was overcome.

Such devotion is not meant only for special Christians such as monastics and hermits of the desert. I find the long, unbroken chain of holy living represented by the monastic tradition to be a help for all. In the last analysis, every Christian must learn a "careful devotion to Christ." We must fast, pray, weep, repent before God, and seek to remember Him moment by moment—and never as an abstraction. Compared to God, *we* are the abstractions. But God has become man, and in that event the abstraction of our schismatic existence was overcome. In the life of the Church we are now united to Reality. Why do we settle for less?

Why are our enemies more important than God? They must be, else we would forgive them in accordance with His commandment. I could take this question and apply it across the board in our Christian lives. God is less important to us than many things, because we believe in the reality of those things more than the Reality of God. It is the habit of two-storey thinking.

Some suggestions, all of which are aimed at overcoming the false sense of God's distance:

1. **Recognize that though "God is everywhere present and filling all things,"** you often go through the world as if He were not particularly present at all and things were just empty things. When you see this, make it a matter of confession and repentance.

2. **Always approach the church and the sacraments** (where we have an even more specific promise of His presence) with awe. Never treat the building or things that have been set aside as holy as though they were common or empty. Do not divide your life into two—"now He's here, now He's not." Syrian Christians traditionally believed that the *Shekinah* presence of God left the Temple and took up abode in the cross—every cross—and thus they had extraordinary devotion to each and every cross. We should never be indifferent to the icon or prayer corner in our home. Cross yourself whenever you pass it or come into its presence.

3. **Make careful preparation for communion.** Always read the pre-communion prayers if you are going to receive communion (and perhaps even if you are not); pray akathists and other devotional prayers that particularly focus on Christ and His presence, such as the Akathist to the Sweetest Lord Jesus. The traditional Western hymn written by St. Patrick, known as his "breastplate," is also a very fine hymn to know. Find it, keep it with you, and learn it.[3]

4. **Learn by heart psalms of presence,** such as Psalm 23, "The Lord is my Shepherd," and Psalm 91, "He who dwells in the secret place of the Most High," and any others that strike you. Repeat them frequently throughout the day.

5. **Throughout the day, search for God.** He is everywhere present, and yet our searching helps us to be more properly aware. In

---

3 The Breastplate of St. Patrick is quoted in *Aidan's Song* by Fr. Aidan Wilcoxson (Conciliar Press, 2010), pp. 59–61.

searching, expect to find Him. He delights in sharing His presence.

6. **Approach others with deep respect and wonder**—it will often be the foundation for love. As much as is possible, forgive everyone for everything, staying mindful of the great mystery that is every human being. If you cannot yet pray for an enemy, begin by saying, "O Lord, do not hold this sin against them on judgment day on my account." It seems to postpone the forgiveness, but it also makes a beginning.

7. **More than anything, give thanks to God for all things.** There is no better way to acknowledge His presence. "In everything give thanks; for this is the will of God in Christ Jesus concerning you" (1 Thess. 5:18).

All of us will stumble and fall frequently in such matters. But we need not abandon ourselves to a Godless world, dotted by oases of His presence. The careful devotion to Christ recognizes Him everywhere—not as in pantheism, but in His goodness and His sustaining of all things, and in His very Person.

The classical Christian tradition of which I have written in this book is not an abstraction, nor should it be taken for one. The consensus of Christianity was strained and broken to a great extent at the time of the Great Schism between East and West, between Roman Catholicism and Eastern Orthodoxy. Though the two still share much common language and understanding, there remains much that separates them. The fragmentation of Protestant Christianity that began with the Reformation in the sixteenth century has only increased in time—with decreasing reference to the classical tradition of the faith. On the other hand, there is a growing movement across the Christian world that recognizes in the classical tradition of the faith the true great wellspring and source of sanity even for modern believers. Any number have even tried their hand at recovering this tradition in one form or another.

I am an Eastern Orthodox Christian priest and bear witness to the living reality of a one-storey faith. This faith abides among us despite the many persecutions it has endured and the temptations of the modern world. I believe that this great treasure of the faith has been preserved according to the promise of God and offers, not the recovery of the classical tradition, but the continuation of that very Tradition in its true and living form. I pray that all who read will be helped to know the God who is everywhere present and filling all things.

And glory to God for all things!

ABOUT THE AUTHOR

Fr. Stephen Freeman is an archpriest in the Orthodox Church in America and serves as pastor of St. Anne Orthodox Church in Oak Ridge, TN. He was educated at Furman University, Seabury-Western Theological Seminary, and Duke University. He is author of the popular blog, *Glory to God for All Things,* and of the weekly podcast, *Glory to God,* on Ancient Faith Radio. He has been deeply involved in mission efforts of the Orthodox Church, particularly in engaging modern culture from within the Tradition of the Church.

 ANCIENT FAITH RADIO

Visit www.ancientfaith.com/podcasts/freeman to listen to episodes of Fr. Stephen's *Glory to God* podcast.

ALSO FROM CONCILAR PRESS

Aidan's Song
A Year in the Life of a Parish Priest
by Fr. Aidan Wilcoxson

Fr. Aidan Wilcoxson describes a year in his life as a parish priest, and as you'll discover, his heart beats full of a contagious joy that spills over into these pages. For those who are curious how a priest spends his time, this book will be enlightening. For those who tend to get discouraged by the daily grind, it will be uplifting. And for all who love to sing to the Lord—literally or figuratively—*Aidan's Song* will definitely have you humming along in praise.
Paperback, 288 pages, ISBN 978-1-936270-03-3, CP No. 007330—$18.95*

A Book of Hours
Meditations on the Traditional Christian Hours of Prayer
by Patricia Colling Egan

Eastern and Western Christians share a rich spiritual heritage in the Hours of Prayer—the brief services of praise and psalmody that mark the progress of each day, sanctifying the hours of our lives. In this gem of a book, Patricia Egan digs deeply into the meaning of each of the Hours, drawing on poetry, nature, experience, and theology to show how the services reflect the different aspects of our salvation and our lives. *A Book of Hours* is an excellent companion for anyone who wants to experience the blessing of praying through the Hours of each day.
Paperback with French flaps, 192 pages, ISBN 978-1-936270-06-4, CP No. 008076—$21.95*

Bread & Water, Wine & Oil
An Orthodox Christian Experience of God
by Fr. Meletios Webber

According to two thousand years of experience, Orthodoxy shows us how to "be transformed by the renewing of our mind"—a process that is aided by participation in the traditional ascetic practices and Mysteries of the Church. In this unique and accessible book, Archimandrite Meletios Webber first explores the role of mystery in the Christian life, then walks the reader through the seven major Mysteries of the Orthodox Church, showing the way to a richer, fuller life in Christ.
Paperback, 200 pages, ISBN: 978-1-888212-91-4, CP No. 006324—$15.95*

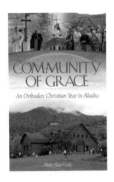

Community of Grace
An Orthodox Christian Year in Alaska
by Mary Alice Cook

Community of Grace is the story of one successful community, made up of the stories of the people who made it happen, and told in the context of the Orthodox worship that binds them all together. Join in the lives of the parishioners of St. John's Orthodox Cathedral in Eagle River, Alaska, as they experience the joys and sorrows, struggles and triumphs of being an intentional community dedicated to life in Christ.
Paperback, 208 pages, ISBN 978-1-936270-07-1, CP No.008077—$17.95*

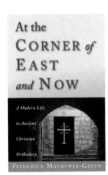

At the Corner of East and Now
A Modern Life in Ancient Christian Orthodoxy
by Frederica Mathewes-Green

Frederica takes us through a typical Divine Liturgy in her little parish of Holy Cross in Baltimore, setting of her well-loved book *Facing East*. Interspersed with reflections on the liturgy and the Orthodox faith are accounts of adventures around the country. In all the places she visits and all the people she meets, Frederica finds insights about faith, American life, and what it means to be human, and she shares these insights with the wit, pathos, and folksy friendliness that have made her one of the most beloved spiritual writers in America.
Paperback, 270 pages, ISBN: 978-1-888212-34-1, CP No. 007609—$16.95*

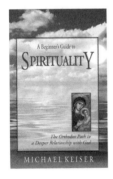

A Beginner's Guide to Spirituality
The Orthodox Path to a Deeper Relationship with God
by Fr. Michael Keiser

Fr. Michael Keiser walks us through the Orthodox Church's timeless teachings and practices on the ancient understanding of Christian spirituality with humor and keen insight. He outlines how ascetic practices, personal and corporate worship, confession and repentance, overcoming the passions, and opening ourselves up to God's grace can lead us to transformation, and to our ultimate destiny— Jerusalem, the heavenly city.
Paperback, 112 pages, ISBN: 978-1-888212-88-4, CP No. 007304—$10.95*

*Plus applicable tax and postage & handling charges. Prices current as of January, 2011. Please call Conciliar Press at 800-967-7377 for complete ordering information, or order online at www.conciliarpress.com.

Visit www.ancientfaithradio.com to listen to podcasts of interest.